Through all the
Changing Scenes of Life

In memory of my Parents
Harry & Elsie
my Brother Harry
and
my Parents-in-Law
Frank & Clara

Through all the
Changing Scenes of Life

"In all your ways acknowledge Him and He will direct your paths."

Proverbs, 3:6

Alan Hunt [signature]

Alan Hunt

*With happy memories of you both
at 'The Kensington'.
from
Alan & Audrey.* [handwritten inscription]

© Alan Hunt 2005

Published by Alan Hunt
68 Coniston Drive
Walton-le-Dale
Preston
Lancashire
PR5 4RQ
Tel: 01772 339554

Quotations from the Holy Bible, unless stated otherwise, are from the
New International Version, and the Acknowledgements of Permissions
to reproduce these and other extracts from copyright sources are to be
found on pages 174 and 175

ISBN 0-9549875-0-0

Printed by
℗ | CPL design+print
348 Station Road
Bamber Bridge
Preston
Lancashire
PR5 6EL
Tel: 01772 335928
Email: sales@cpl-design-print.co.uk

Registered charities will benefit from the sale of this book

THE PROLOGUE

Through all the changing scenes of life,
In trouble and in joy,
The praises of my God shall still,
My heart and tongue employ.

O magnify the Lord with me,
With me exalt His Name;
When in distress to Him I called,
He to my rescue came.

O make but trial of His love,
Experience will decide,
How blest are they, and only they,
Who in His truth confide.

(From words written in 1696 by Nahum Tate 1652-1715
and Nicholas Brady 1639-1726)

On the morning of Sunday the 9th of March 2003, I began the sermon in St Leonard's Church, Walton-le-Dale, by saying, "One of the experiences which is so true of life for so many, is that one moment they can feel on top of the world, filled and thrilled with excitement and elation, and the next they wonder what has hit them, as without warning, or as the King James Version of the Bible would have it 'in the twinkling of an eye', their world has fallen apart and they are plunged into the depths of doubt, even of despair; a situation and an experience so hard to cope with as the world becomes a very lonely and desolate place." As I was saying these words, I little realised how soon they would become a living reality for me, for just thirteen days later, in the early hours of the 22nd of March, I awoke with excruciating pain in my right side, from which I could find no relief until one hour later I was given a pain killing injection by the emergency doctor, who then called for the ambulance and arranged for my admission to hospital, for what turned out to be major surgery. The events of the next few hours are somewhat blurred, but I remember many questions being asked and X-rays being taken, in order to try and determine the root cause of the problem; I also have recollections of work being carried out on my spine in preparation for the epidural injections which were to control the post-operative pain, and from then on nothing more until I became aware of voices attempting to restrain me from trying to remove the ventilator tubes from my mouth, as seemingly I had been expected to be dependent on the ventilator for some considerable time. I was also aware of familiar voices, before hearing, for the first time, the voice of the Consultant Surgeon Mr.J.B.Ward, who quietly told me what he had already told my family earlier, that when he opened me up he had found a growth which was attached to my liver, gall bladder and bowel. On top of the growth was an abscess which had burst and which had been the cause of all the pain; consequently before proceeding it had been necessary, first of all, to wash out all the pus in order to avoid further complications and this had resulted in quite a lot of blood and fluid loss. This being done he had then proceeded to remove part of my liver, my gall bladder completely and then to carry out a bowel re-section or re-plumbing as he termed it. He also assured me that he had removed every trace of the growth and that depending on the results of laboratory tests any other precautionary treatment would be sorted out later.

Even in my hazy state of mind, this was enough to tell me that I had been very fortunate indeed, and that the intense pain which I had suffered was in fact a blessing in disguise, in alerting us to the serious problem that had been quietly developing inside, and which, had it been left undisturbed, could have led to even more serious consequences later. What the future held and what laboratory tests would reveal was something only time would tell, and for the moment, to be free from pain was wonderful; sleep beckoned and I had no resistance to it.

I awoke to the busyness of intensive care with its many comings and goings and checks on this and that. I was especially fortunate to have Amanda as my key nurse, and I will be forever grateful to her for her loving care, and for her wonderful words of encouragement, interspersed with her often mischievous sense of humour, all of which meant so much to me in my hour of need.

After so much attention, it came as something of a shock to be transferred to a general surgical ward, where one initially felt a real sense of vulnerability, despite being assured by the staff that this was only to be expected after major surgery. The worst time being during the night when there was only a minimum staff of three or four to cope with three wards and two side rooms;

but the challenge had to be faced. The physiotherapists wasted no time in encouraging me to take my first unsteady and faltering steps together with all the support appendages; they also showed me the most effective way to move from a prone to an upright position which proved a real blessing, and they also showed me the best way to deal with coughing and sneezing as painlessly as possible. There were also instructions with regard to the necessary exercises for hands and feet in order to maintain good circulation and the importance of not crossing feet and legs.

So began the first and often uncertain steps towards recovery, but on the whole the staff seemed quite amazed at the progress I made; there was also the added bonus of visits from loved ones and friends, the assurance of good wishes and prayerful support from so many by telephone, and a steady stream, amounting eventually to one hundred and twenty, get well cards. All of which helped so much and particularly when there were problems to be dealt with. First of all it was discovered that there was a possible threat of an infection from the drain in my stomach travelling around my right side towards the epidural site in the spine. It was early days, and the staff were loathe to do so, but such an infection could not be risked, and the epidural site had to be dismantled and we had to revert to oral pain control, which wasn't easy because I still had a tube down my throat, but thankfully it proved satisfactory. After several days of nil by mouth except for small quantities of water, I was told that I could now graduate to small quantities of food and an increased fluid intake. I must confess that after days of watching other patients enjoying their food, it was good to be able to partake with them, and I can truthfully say that I did not overdo it, but after two days I felt decidedly unwell and was violently sick. I was immediately put to bed and back on to a fluid drip and nil by mouth. I felt devastated, as from previous drips my body was already like that of Mr.Blobby, and the probability of even more fluid retention certainly added to the increasing pressures of the situation. During that night, in the early hours of the morning, I felt very low indeed, and prayed earnestly for Divine help. It was then that I glanced up to my drip to find that it had stopped; I called for one of the nurses who tried in vain to get it started, and then said he would have to send for a doctor to insert another line. This doctor was an Indian lady who was very kind and sympathetic, but in spite of three attempts, because of the swollen condition of my arms and hands, she was unable to locate a vein! Her next words to me were like music to my ears, "I'm so sorry to have caused you all this discomfort, but I'm afraid we will have to revert to plan number two, and that is to put you back on fluids by mouth in the hope that you will be able to keep them down for the next twenty four hours so that then you will not need any drip!" Praise the Lord, my prayer had been answered, and after giving heartfelt thanks, and enjoying a nice drink of water, I fell asleep with the deep feeling that all would be well. It seems that what had happened was that the natural response of the stomach to being handled during surgery is to paralyse itself for its own protection. Consequently the re-introduction of food to the system, albeit in small amounts can, and did, result in the sickness I had suffered. However all's well that ends well and after a further forty-eight hours I was able to resume eating without further problems, and with the re-plumbed bowel also functioning well and the surgical team more than satisfied with progress, the only question mark now was over the outstanding findings of the laboratory from their examination of the 'bits and pieces' that had been forwarded to them for analysis.

The results arrived after eight days and when Mr. Ward's Registrar came to see me his expression gave nothing away, and as he sat on the bed next to me, something said 'is this the moment of truth'? It was. "Well, Mr. Hunt, we have had your results back and I can only say it is good news, there is no cancer"! My wife Audrey, daughter Janet and I were overjoyed, and there were tears of relief as we gave thanks to God for yet another answer to many prayers from us and from hundreds more besides. It was obviously not the result they had been expecting, but they still shared our joy and relief. When I asked about any further treatment, he said "forget it, just go home and get well; how does the day after tomorrow sound to you?" The following morning, when Mr. Ward called on his rounds, he smiled broadly and said, "what about the results eh? - Somebody up there is certainly looking after you!" "Yes" I replied, " they certainly are; but I do believe in miracles and I hope that after this you will do too." Again he smiled broadly, and as he walked away the expression on his face spoke volumes.

In the afternoon of the following day, the 3rd of April, I left hospital for home, and the day afterwards Audrey and I celebrated our Golden Wedding Anniversary, quietly and with thanksgiving, both very much aware that it could have been a very different story.

Experiences such as these, are bound, by their very nature, not only to leave one with a profound sense of thanksgiving to Almighty God for His love and healing power, but also with a deep desire to share them with others, in the sincere hope that they too will find them of help in their own time of need, or as a means of broadening and deepening their own faith and understanding of life, prayer, healing and discipleship. Moreover the acute sense of the slenderness of the thread of life, and the certainty of one's own mortality, convinced me that the time to put my thoughts and intentions over many years into words, needed to commence as soon as possible. They are dedicated, with love and thanksgiving, to my Lord and Saviour Jesus Christ, and to my Wife and our family, for their love, understanding and patience over the years, very conscious of the words of the late Dr. William Barclay in his final work 'Testament of Faith', "Home is the place where they know us at our worst, and still love us."

CHAPTER ONE

In the popular musical version of 'Les Misérables', one of the principal characters Jean Valjean is found in a real dilemma. For the past nineteen years he has been imprisoned for the relatively petty crime of breaking a windowpane and stealing a loaf of bread. As prisoner 24601 he has been under the watchful eye of Inspector Javert as his chief captor, and the man responsible for his initial arrest. As such there is no love lost between them. At the end of the nineteenth year Valjean is given parole, which he sees as the ideal opportunity to begin a new life. He breaks parole, changes his name, and although pursued by the implacable Javert, he rises to become a factory owner and the Mayor of Montreuil-sur-Mer. All goes well until one of his factory workers by the name of Fantine gets herself into trouble. She has a young daughter and having been deserted by the father of the child, she has been forced to sell what few possessions she has, before resorting against her will to prostitution in order to make ends meet. She gets into a fight with a prospective customer, and is about to be taken to prison by Inspector Javert, when the Mayor arrives and demands that she be taken to hospital instead. The Mayor then rescues a man who has been pinned down by a runaway cart. Javert has an extremely good memory and this rescue reminds him of the abnormal strength of prisoner 24601, a man he thinks has just been recaptured. and now awaits trial. Despite the temptation to do nothing about it Valjean is unable to see an innocent man go to prison in his place, and so we find him facing up to his true identity and asking himself the question, which is the reason for my having told you the story thus far, WHO AM I? It is the question I believe all of us who are seeking to come to terms with life, what it has meant thus far, what it means for us now, and what it can mean for the future, need to be asking. It will help us to face up to our true identity which, although it may, or may not, be the identity others know and have known us by over the years, will nevertheless be the one which really matters, in that it is the identity by which we are known to the One to whom all hearts are open, all desires are known and from whom no secrets are hidden. For Jean Valjean it meant that despite all the danger and the consequences for himself and his future, and the futures of all those in his employment, he had to be true to himself and everything his past had taught him, and so he went to court and revealed his own identity. He then hurried from the astonished courtroom, leaving behind him an innocent man in the dock with no case against him, and Javert back to square one!

For all of us, such self and soul searching, painful though it so often can prove to be, is not only a recognition of the importance of the maxim 'to your own self be true', but also a real and positive step toward getting our priorities in order and in acknowledging our deepest need, which, in a strict Christian interpretation of life, is that of being in a right relationship with God, in and through His Beloved Son, our Lord and Saviour Jesus Christ; it is also to establish the bed rock upon which all our thinking on, and understanding of, life, prayer, healing and discipleship will rest, and from which it will gain inspiration and the loving sense of urgency, through the power and guidance of the Holy Spirit, which will not only lead us into all truth and help us to grow into the fullness and stature of Christ, but will also enable us, in love and gratitude, to encourage others to do the same.

At the outset it has to be acknowledged that, as individuals, we are all coming to this special time in our lives from different angles and walks of life, all of which are threads embroidered into the rich tapestry of life; experiences, some of which we would rather forget, but also others which are very precious, and amongst them times when, please God, we have felt Him near, or from hindsight can see a pattern in our life in which in a very real sense we see His guiding hand, even though we may not have felt it at the time.

It is such eventualities and experiences that need to form a real part in our prayers of thanksgiving to Almighty God, and in our asking Him to enable us to see Him more clearly, to love Him more dearly, and to follow Him more nearly, day by day. So we begin the story of my own pilgrimage from birth until now.

I was born on Sunday the 5th of May 1931, as the second son of Harry and Elsie Hunt, both of whom were employed in Calvert's Mill in the village of Walton-le dale, Preston, Lancashire, where I was born at 45 Chorley Road; which for those interested in history, local and otherwise, is situated immediately opposite the then Unicorn Inn where reputedly Oliver Cromwell stayed at the time of the Battle of Preston in the August of 1648. My birth, however, was to cause no such stir except for the family, in that I was born with a Cleft Palate and Hare Lip, which meant that from the age of three months up to being seven years old, I had to spend long periods in Pendlebury Children's Hospital in Manchester undergoing corrective surgery. It was a hard and difficult time for my parents and big brother Harry, and I will always be grateful to them and particularly to my Mother for all the love and devotion which saw me through those years and afterwards as well.

I was raised in a Christian, but not over religious, home where I was taught to say my prayers, and grew to accept Sunday School and Church as part of family life just as much as attending St Leonard's Day School.

When I was nine or ten years old, I wasn't particularly ear-wigging, but I overheard my mother telling someone about the circumstances of my birth, and how she had such a difficult time that when I was delivered I was laid to one side whilst the Doctor, for whom she also worked as a part- time dispenser, and the midwife whom she knew well, attended to her. I was lying with my back to them and when, very soon afterwards, they turned me around and saw the extent of the problem, my mother heard one of them say, "what shall we do with him"? She then went on to add, "and if he hadn't begun to cry at that moment I don't think he would be here now". I know I was only a youngster, but I do remember thinking, 'but I am still here, so there must be a reason'; well I didn't know it then, but obviously God had other plans for me!!

At school I was only average, and when at eleven years of age I took the entrance examination for the Grammar School, I failed; which in retrospect could have proved a relief to my parents with very little money in the house. But their relief would have been short lived, because two years later I passed the entrance examination to the Junior Technical School of the Harris Institute in Preston where my full-time education continued for a further two years.

There is a saying that schooldays are the happiest days of your life, and there is no doubt this has proved true for a lot of people, but I have to confess that it never felt true for me, in fact so far as I was concerned, they could not come to an end quickly enough. This is not to cast any slur on those whose sad lot it was to have to try to teach me, it was just that I had no real natural talent and consequently it was all a matter of hard slogging in order to obtain reasonable standards and requirements.

But whilst I may not have had the natural talents as regards ability, I was never afraid of hard work and this remained the norm throughout my academic life; and it was to be given a boost from a very unexpected source when, at the age of fourteen I was Confirmed, in St Leonard's Church on March the 9th 1946, by the then Bishop of Blackburn, Dr.Askwith, who gave us as our Confirmation Text to remember, the words of St Paul's letter to the Philippians chapter 1 verse 6, "Being confident of this very thing, that He which hath begun a good work in you, will perform it until the day of Jesus

Christ" (King James Version); words which like a golden thread have been a real source both of comfort and inspiration through all the changing scenes of life.

Whilst being well aware of the fact that Pride is listed as the first of the seven deadly sins, I have no hesitation in saying that I am proud of the fact that I was born into a working class family and environment. It taught me a great deal about human nature and the importance of community, about mutual responsibility and interdependence, about caring and sharing what little we had with others in time of need, in being there for each other whenever and wherever the need arose, and of course in many other ways as well. All of which has not only enabled me to be intensely grateful for a background which has kept my feet firmly rooted in the real world, but also for one that has been a measuring rod for my thoughts and prayers with regard to the future of our modern day world, where so many of the caring and sharing attitudes I grew up with, find little or no place, and where self, selfishness and greed are all too prevalent.

All of which brings me to the next phase in my education, when, after completing my time at the Harris Institute and having obtained an average leaving certificate, I began an Engineering Apprenticeship with Messrs Leyland Motors Limited, at that time one of the foremost heavy goods vehicle manufacturers in this country, with exports to Europe and beyond, together with manufacturing and assembly agreements with countries such as Israel, Spain, India and even 'down-under' in Australia. Consequently, it was a great privilege to be able to work for such a well-established and notable company, with so much to offer those willing to work hard; and together with the lessons learned as a result of my working class background, my new life and work on the shop floor of industry also had much to teach me in what I choose to call 'the University of Life.' As a boy in a man's world I not only had to cope with a new way of life and work, but also amongst other things with the bad language and references to sexual experiences and prowess, which although every day and amusing to those concerned, were nevertheless not a good example either to me or to others similarly placed. Those concerned obviously saw this as part of our 'education' and preparation for greater things without thought for any psychological damage it could cause. But such is life in a far from perfect world, and whilst at the time I found it difficult to cope with, it did enable me to begin to see what makes certain people tick, and ultimately I came to realise that it was all part of my preparation for a future ministry, where so often, it is the men-folk who are so difficult to reach. As such, I have found my engineering background as a whole to be of tremendous help, in being able, in effect, to speak in the kind of language they understand and are able to identify with, metaphorically speaking of course!

In 1950, after having had one or two girlfriends along the way, I fell for one particular young lady with whom I had in fact grown up. Audrey Sharples was in a higher class than me in St Leonard's Day School, but we were in the same class in Sunday School, and there were many times, so I was told subsequently, when she went home and complained bitterly to her parents about my behaviour, - which, as you will hear in more detail later on, left much to be desired - consequently it came as a surprise, not least to her parents Frank and Clara and to many others as well when later we became a couple. We became engaged in 1952, and were married in St Leonard's Church on the 4th of April 1953, and even though the events of 22nd March 2003 caused some real concern, we have now passed our half - century, not out!

Our first daughter Janet Margaret was born on the 5th of April 1958, and after a rather difficult pregnancy, her safe arrival was the cause of great thanksgiving from us all. Two years earlier however, something happened which was to lead to a new adventure for all of us. Along with other members, I attended a meeting of St.Leonard's Men's Society. The guest speaker that particular evening was Canon Stanley Picton the Parish Priest at St.George's Church in Preston. St.George's was, and still is, in the Anglo-Catholic tradition, and amongst the many topics covered in the talk was the practice of making the sign of the Cross and its meaning for different people. The speaker was not referring to its use in Holy Baptism, or in the Blessing of the Elements in Holy Communion, or indeed, in the Blessing of people, but rather in the personal sense by individuals for a variety of reasons. As Fr.Picton quite rightly pointed out, so personal were these, he could only speak for himself and what it meant for him. As he saw it, it meant making the letter "I" and then crossing it out (+). A very simple explanation and yet, at the same time, a very profound one containing a great deal of food for thought. In a very real sense it was, in the first instance, his acknowledgement that before the Cross of Jesus he was a sinner standing in the need of grace, and the act of crossing out himself was his acknowledgement of his deepest need, and a willingness to make soul-searching a real priority, in endeavouring, not only to seek to draw near to the Throne of Grace and to acknowledge Jesus Christ as his Lord and Saviour, but also to taking a positive step toward making his faith in Him a living reality in a life of service for Him in the world from thereon; every subsequent 'crossing' being a reminder of that special time in his life and the need for constant renewal. Prior to this Audrey and I had been members of the Church Choir and I had been a bell-ringer and a member of the Parochial Church Council for some considerable time, but that night as I travelled home from the Men's Society Meeting, and thought about all that Fr.Picton had shared with us, I became very aware that something more had to be done. It wasn't akin to St.Paul's experience on the road to Damascus, there was no blinding flash or voice from heaven, but the feeling within me was real and without doubt, and I will always remember, the quiet starlit night on the road to Bamber Bridge and the knowledge that I had to offer myself to the Church in whatever way She felt I could be of use. When I reached home I shared with Audrey all that had happened and the following Sunday after Church I did the same with our Vicar, the Reverend John.L.Brook. It was as if he already knew and was expecting me, and without any hesitation undertook responsibility for helping me to test what he believed was my vocation, in preparing me to become a Licensed Reader as a first step along the road to its possible fulfilment. John was a Yorkshire man who had been a chemist in Bradford before training for the Sacred Ministry and subsequent Ordination. He was an excellent teacher and communicator and very painstaking in the way he prepared for our study sessions, first of all in one of the classrooms in St Leonard's School and later in the vicarage. I also have fond memories of the savoury toasties that Mrs Brook always prepared for us afterwards. John not only gave me a thorough grounding in the subjects set by the Central Readers Board, but also in the right and proper way in which to prepare for, and conduct, divine worship, in preaching, in reading aloud the Holy Scriptures and in administering the Sacrament of Holy Communion with due awe and reverence. I shall be forever grateful for his wisdom, his kind words and his advice, that I not only remember with deep respect, but which are a real part of me as a lasting memorial to him and his dear wife Joyce. There are of course many examples, but perhaps one will suffice; "Always remember Alan, that when people kneel to receive the Blessed Sacrament of Holy Communion, the only things they see of you are your hands and your feet and it is vitally important that your hands and particularly your nails, like your shoes, should always be clean."

Thinking of these words always reminds me of the story of the two old ladies standing outside church and discussing the service that had just ended.

In the main they had enjoyed it, the hymns were well known and very sing-able, the prayers had been well prepared and were sincere and helpful, but what about the sermon? This particular morning the preacher had not gone to the pulpit, but instead had stood at the top of the chancel steps in full view of the congregation. For quite a while all went well and he had their full attention, then it had all gone wrong, for no longer were they paying attention. Why? Because they had both noticed that he was wearing dirty shoes. A very timely reminder to all of us, to take care and to remember that what we are, can so often speak much louder than what we say!

After two years in training as a Postulant, I was Licensed as a Reader in Blackburn Cathedral by the then Bishop, Walter Baddeley, in Advent 1958, and took up my duties in St.Leonard's Church. In a sermon I preached the following year, I said that as the disciples of Jesus in the world, we must be ready and willing to follow wherever he might lead us, in order to do His will. A few days later, I was invited by my employers to go out to the then Madras in South India for two years, as Adviser to Planning and Production in the manufacturing and assembly plant at Ennore, approximately twenty miles north of the city. It was one of those instances where, on the one hand, there was the recognition that we would need time to talk it over as a family, and, on the other, the need for an answer tomorrow! . There was not much time, but we decided that whilst neither of us relished the idea of being apart, it could be a big help to us financially for the future, no matter what the future might hold, and after much rather hurried thought and prayer, it was decided that I would accept the challenge. But why choose me? In retrospect, I suppose, they felt that as a married man who was involved in the Church, I could have a steadying influence on the other Leyland Technicians who were already there; also that as a man of letters, that is of engineering qualifications, together with all the training and experience I had in Jig and Tool design and manufacturing techniques, made me the prime contender for the job. Whether they were right, remained to be seen; it was a risk they, and we, had to take!

Perhaps at this point, dear reader, you may wish to take me to task about my being a man of letters when previously I declared that, academically, I was only average! Well, I still stand by what I said. After joining Leyland Motors my studies continued in part-time day courses and evening classes; and eventually I obtained both Ordinary and Higher National Certificates in Mechanical and Production Engineering and later became a Graduate of both the Institute of Mechanical Engineers and the Institute of Production

Engineers. But I do not see these apparent successes in terms of academic ability, but rather, as I said earlier, in terms of genuine hard work, together with a good memory and a good sense of humour, all of which added up to my being a good examination candidate. I trust that this explanation will help to clear up the apparent contradiction, and enable us to move on.

The journey to India, my first by air, was in a Super Constellation of Air India International, by way of Paris, Rome, Cairo, Beirut and Bombay. I enjoyed the experience, but found it a little scary at times. The aircraft had four propellers and when these were 'feathered' they almost appeared to stop, and when it was dark the occasional flames from the engine exhausts were also unnerving; but I consoled myself with the thought that the pilot and crew were as anxious to reach our destination safely as we the passengers were! I also met two very interesting fellow passengers. The first was a young man, a Christian from Uganda who was travelling to Australia. We shared a lot about our lives, our families, our work and not least our faith. One could not help but be impressed by his sincerity and his simple faith which was inspiring to say the least, and although I only had the pleasure of his company for the best part of two days, the impact of our meeting left an indelible mark on my life. In sharp contrast to this was my meeting with one of India's legends of the silver screen, Raj Kapoor, world renowned actor, director and producer, who, when compared with my Ugandan brother, had enjoyed the very best that his world status had brought his way. But despite his exalted position in the film industry, success had not gone to his head. On a one to one basis he was a very ordinary, likeable and friendly man. Whenever he was in Madras at one of the many film studios, he always stayed in the Oceanic Hotel where I also lived and was always pleased to see me. I suppose it also helped that I had an alcohol licence and therefore he was able to have a few home comforts; all unofficially of course!

I don't think I will ever forget setting foot on South Indian soil for the first time; my thoughts were very much in keeping with those of John Henry Newman in his well known hymn, 'Lead kindly light', written at one of the most difficult times in his own life; for me too 'the night was dark and I was far from home' and I too was praying earnestly 'hold Thou my feet, I do not ask to see the distant scene, one step enough for me'.

At that particular time, the population of the City of Madras was approximately three million, and so it seemed hardly likely that one extra would ever have been noticed, and yet, it was just over a week after my arrival that I had a message asking me to contact the Reverend Ian Calvert who was the Chaplain of St.George's Cathedral. As a result of that meeting I was granted authority by the Bishop, to officiate as a Lay Preacher in any Pastorate of the Diocese of Madras on the invitation of the Presbyter concerned, but particularly in the Pastorate of the Cathedral group of Pastorates. In addition to the Cathedral this included St.Mary's Church in the Fort St.George, where Robert Clive was governor and which housed the old East India Company. Clive and his wife were married in St.Mary's, which remained the British Community Church. Also in the Cathedral group, was St.Thomas's English Church, a smaller Indian Parish Church in the district of Mylapore, not far from the Oceanic Hotel. Now, whilst all of this in itself was an exciting prospect, it was made doubly so by the fact that I was now at the very heart of the Church of South India, which meant that in addition to the above I also had the opportunity of taking services and preaching in churches of other traditions, for example the Methodist, the Presbyterian and, on the two Good Fridays I was there, in the Baptist Church as well.

During my stay I met many lovely people. I have already mentioned Ian Calvert; he and Mary were very kind, and whenever I was invited to visit them in the evening after dark, I had to stay in the car until the bearers came with torches and long poles to clear away the snakes, and the same procedure when I left. Suffice it to say that one did not arrive unexpected! In church at home, I had always worn a black cassock and white surplice, but in South India cassocks were also white, so that when I first appeared on duty I was in borrowed 'plumes'. The following day I went down to see one of the many tailors in the bazaars and asked him to make me a set identical to the one I had taken. However, I had not counted on him following my instructions exactly to the letter; the samples I had given him had seen a lot of service and had the odd patch, so had the new ones, they even had blank labels in the backs of the garments where the original maker's labels had been!!! Consequently there were many smiles when I showed them to Ian, and I think we both learned from the experience. Another experience I will never forget, was that of taking part in the Madras Musical Society's production of Gilbert and Sullivan's, 'The Mikado'; the cast of which came from near and far and was full of real 'characters'. It was also representative of all walks of life; all of them lovely people and a pleasure to be with, and to work with. It was only to be expected that most of the leading parts would be taken by local actors and singers, after all it was their society and the rest of us were really only making up the numbers. The one exception was the part of the Lord High Executioner taken by the Reverend Peter Cochrane, a Methodist Minister. He was an absolute 'scream' and brought real and lasting enjoyment to all concerned.

Someone else I will never forget is the Rev.Dr.Thomas Sitther, a South Indian priest, as black as they come, with a voice like gravel, a lovely disposition, and always full of encouragement. I first met him at St.Thomas' Church, not named after him of course, where we shared in many services together. Such was his keenness to keep me involved in the service of Holy Communion that in only a little while he had me do virtually everything apart from the Absolution, the Words of Consecration, and the Final Blessing. Such was his enthusiasm to care and to share that it was contagious, and consequently became a real part of me. Surely, I was experiencing here at first hand, what Christianity is, and should be, all about. One day we were shocked to hear the news that Thomas's wife had died very suddenly and unexpectedly and, as was the custom, because of the heat, the funeral was held the same day and was followed a few days later by a memorial service. I am afraid that I do not remember where that service was held, but I do know that it was extremely well attended and certainly charged with emotion, especially when the time came for the sermon and who should go to the pulpit but Thomas himself. He began by saying "You may all find it very strange, even peculiar, that I should be the one to preach at this very sad time, but who better, who else knew my dear wife better than I did?" Who indeed, and as he continued to share with us his innermost thoughts of the one he had loved and still loved so dearly, there was not a dry eye in the place. He had given us all much food for thought even though it must have been painful to him, and we all loved and respected him for it. His words taught me a great deal as regards funerals and how they should always be conducted with dignity, respect and sensitivity for all concerned, and that, although it may be very demanding in terms of time and energy, there is no substitute for real involvement, for it is only when we share in the pain that the doors in the hearts and minds of those who are listening and searching, will be opened. Furthermore, just as Thomas, in his own way, was able and willing to use the occasion of his own sudden and unexpected loss to challenge all of us to take stock of our lives, and to get our priorities in order, in so doing he was also underlining, for all with ears to hear, the importance of using such an occasion as an evangelistic opportunity, with the emphasis as always on sensitivity.

Another character I want to mention is Mr.French, the Verger at the

Cathedral, who was always pleasant and helpful and who always had a twinkle in his eyes. I always remember the first time I was preaching in the Cathedral, because as I arrived, the first person I met was Mr.French carrying the Bishop's crosier- the Sunday name for his crook-"yes Mr.Hunt, he has come to listen to you", and quite suddenly I felt not a little apprehensive; and it must have shown, because he said "don't worry I'm sure all will go well". My text that night was from St.Paul's Letter to the Romans Chapter 5 verse 1, "Therefore being justified by faith, we have peace with God through our Lord Jesus Christ", and as I was preaching, I rather sensed the Bishop's gaze and possibly the odd shake of the Episcopal head. After the service, all those involved in it usually went to the main door to say goodbye to the departing congregation. This being done, I made my way back to the vestry to be met once more by Mr.French. "Is his Lordship still here?" I asked. "No, he's gone home, so he must be satisfied, otherwise you would have known about it in no uncertain terms!" I have always been grateful that he told me that after my sermon and not before. I think it was all part of his being a very caring person; I never knew his Christian name, but had I to give him one it would certainly be Barnabas, 'Son of encouragement'.

One family I used to visit quite regularly were the West's, who lived in the centre of the city. They, like Mr.French, were Anglo-Indian, and by western standards quite poor; but they were always welcoming and appreciative of a visit. Their daughter Yvonne was a regular worshipper at St.Mary's Church, and whenever I was there I would give her a lift home, which is how I came to know the family in the first place. Mr.West, -whose Christian Name I never knew either- knew the Bible literally front to back, having read it in its entirety over thirty times; such that he could 'run rings' around me - in the nicest possible taste of course- and I will be forever in his debt for stirring up in me a longing to know the Bible as well as he did; a longing which I am still working hard to achieve, but enjoying every minute in the process.

Toward the end of February 1961, there was a State Visit to Madras by Her Majesty the Queen and H.R.H.Prince Philip. As part of their tour of the various places of interest, they paid a visit to the Fort St.George and to St.Mary's Church, where I was invited to robe and to stand with the rest of the clergy just outside the main door. The Bishop in Madras, (note, in not of) the Rt.Rev.David Chellappa, who was not particularly well at the time, was seated not far from me and in a quiet time he called me over and said, "I was just thinking Hunt, whenever I see you dressed up like that, I don't know whether

I am looking at a wolf in sheep's clothing or a sheep in wolf's clothing." I smiled at him and said, "I'm sorry Bishop, but I am afraid it is a risk you will have to take." His reply rather took me by surprise, "It is a risk I am more than happy to take. I have Authorised and Commissioned you, and were you staying on in India I would be more than happy to Ordain you as well." How different the attitude here was compared with home, with a minimum of red tape, and how nice to be surrounded by sincere encouragement, rather than the lack of it, that I was to experience in the future.

Such then, are some of the precious memories I have of my two years in South India; an experience which taught me so much, and which I would not have wanted to miss for the world. I only wish that Audrey and Janet could have been there to share it all with me, but alas it was not possible and I can only hope that now I have committed my memories to paper, this may in some small way redress the apparent unfairness of it all. My one regret was the sudden death of my Dad in September 1960, just fourteen months after I left home. I will always remember his words on the day I left; he took me to one side and said, "If you had the chance to come home half-way through your two years, would you?" I didn't hesitate to reply "yes of course," little knowing what my reason for coming home would be! Nor will I ever forget returning from work to the Oceanic Hotel on that Thursday night, when the person on reception handed me two things. The first was the "football post" which Dad sent to me every week during the season, usually with a written message somewhere on the front page; the second was the telegram telling me of his sudden death! It was a great shock, as it has been for many before me and many since, and as I busied myself contacting work and setting in motion arrangements for returning home, which was part of my contract, several times my mind went to dear old Thomas Sitther and the things we learned from his sermon; and especially so when I also had to contact Ian Calvert at the Cathedral, so that he could make alternative arrangements to cover services I was due to conduct. Because of the circumstances, and following the advice of the undertakers, by the time I arrived home late on the Saturday, the funeral had already taken place; which I also found very difficult; but a friend of ours had taken photographs which helped a great deal and allowed me, along with visits to his grave, to say what I needed to say to the one whose veiled 'prophecy' had come true and had brought me home. Yes, it was a sad time but the month at home was good for us as a family and did break up the two years of separation; but in another way, after my return to India at the request of the Company, the rest of the time seemed more difficult and to pass more slowly. If you were to ask me what lessons my Dad's passing taught me, I would say that it underlined the importance of loving and cherishing our loved ones all that we can whilst we have them with us, and also to listen very carefully to everything they have to say, because we never know if those words will be the last they say to us. It also underlined yet again the uncertainty of life and the need to say all we need to say and to do all that we need to do, whilst we can.

Although as mentioned above the remainder of my time in India did tend to pass slowly, pass it did, and at the end of June 1961 I returned home to the family and resumed work with the Leyland parent company, and two years later our second daughter Linda Jane was born safely at home, again with much thanksgiving. In the same year I was also invited to join the Whalley Abbey Ordination Course for older men, which involved a lot of reading at home, together with meetings and the odd residential weekend, under the care and guidance of Rev.Canon Wilfrid Browning, the then Canon Theologian of the Diocese and Warden of the Abbey. All of this proved rather heavy going, but in the end well worthwhile, for in July 1964, I received a letter from the Revd. Basil Cornish, Chairman of the Central Advisory Council for the Ministry, inviting me to a Selection Conference to be held from August 17th-20th at Stone in Staffordshire. It proved a very interesting and enlightening experience for several reasons, not least in meeting others, who like me, were coming to a point of decision in their lives; a decision to be made by others in the name of the Church. There were times when I felt uneasy, and somewhat inferior, because the majority of them were openly admitting that, without doubt, they felt an unmistakable call to the Priesthood, whereas I for my part had no such claim to make. However, any misgivings I had were soon allayed when I once again came to terms with the fact that, after all, this was a selection conference and that I was offering myself to serve in whatever capacity Mother Church felt best. The selection panel was made up mainly of clergy with one layman, and one by one we were summoned for interview. As these progressed, it transpired that for the great majority of the candidates, - I think there were about twenty of us altogether - the most difficult one to cope with was the layman. Was this, I wondered, a sign of things to come, in that I had no problems with him at all. But this did not mean that I did not have any problems, for my stumbling block, albeit temporary, came with my interview with the then Chaplain of Pembroke College Oxford and Professor of Medieval History. The interview, which proved to be very short, began in silence as he read through the details of my application. This being duly done, his opening remark to me went something like this "I see Mr Hunt that from an academic point of view you have nothing to offer to the Church, so why are you here". My initial reaction was to realise that whatever engineering qualifications I had meant nothing to this man, who was either an intellectual snob, or so steeped in history as to be completely out of touch with the real world. I also wondered how our Lord, as a humble carpenter from Nazareth, would have fared in this situation! Then, after a short time of quiet and more charitable reflection, I gave him my reply, " I am here for two reasons, the first being that I love God, and the second, that I love His children." He looked at me in a way that told me that such a reply had not been expected, slowly closed his folder, and said, "Well, I certainly cannot think of any two better reasons; but before you go, (I had only just sat down) tell me, what will you do if we turn you down?" "I will think and pray about it, and if I think you are wrong, I will come back again!" Shortly after the conference, the Diocesan Chaplain for Ordinands contacted me with the news that in one of the shortest reports they had ever received, I had been accepted as a suitable candidate for training. The Chaplain, Rev.Canon Schofield, then went on to say that the problems with regard to the financing of my time in theological college from the family point of view, still needed to be resolved before any further progress could be made. Applications to various sources had proved fruitful and there was no problem regarding the first year, it was the second year that was the difficult one. Audrey and I did have some savings, and after much thought and prayer, we decided we should go ahead in faith, knowing that it could leave us with virtually nothing.

It was decided that I should do my training at St.Michael and All Angels Theological College, Llandaff, where it was felt that I would see Anglicanism at its best in the Church of Wales! My two years course began in October 1965, and although I had originally intended to do an Essay course, the Warden, Fr.O.G.Rees, always known affectionately, and with his self-conscious approval as Og (from Psalms 135 verse 11 and 136 verse 20), suggested that I took instead the recognised General Ordination Examination, which he felt would ultimately give me more satisfaction. In retrospect, I am sure he was right, but at the time I was not so sure, because although the work content would have been approximately the same, I was now to be faced, yet again, with having to sit written examinations, which, after several years out of practice was not easy. However, it had to be done, and although I did not break any pots, I managed to pass both years without any need for re-sits. I will always be grateful to the staff for their help and guidance, indeed, looking back, I certainly would not have envied them their job. Fr.Rees, although decorated for bravery during World War Two, was in many ways a saintly man. He taught us Church History and was always very patient. He was also a very caring and loving man, who, along with Mrs.Rees, 'Auntie Lil', was always there in time of need. He was very supportive indeed when, only a month after beginning college, my father-in-law Frank died very suddenly, and he also gave me every assistance in a struggle I had with the diocese concerning an award I had received from the Lancashire Education Authority. Prior to going to college I had not applied to the L.E.A. for a grant because I understood that they did not support theological students. However, once at college, it was suggested by a fellow student that I gave it a try, after all, as mentioned earlier, financially, we were in need of help, particularly with the second year. Much to my joy and relief, they came up trumps and made me a grant of £275 per year plus fees. I duly reported this news to our Director of Ordinands Canon Schofield, and in reply he said "It is good to hear that your application to the County Education Authority has borne such prolific fruit. I am afraid, however, that this means that your CACTM (Church's Advisory Council for the Ministry) grant will be reduced from £400 to £17 per annum." His letter closed with 'congratulations on the success of an application, which materially benefits the funds of the Church.' I felt disgusted and devastated and immediately went to see Fr.Rees, whose initial response was to contact the Director of Education for Lancashire, Mr.Percy Lord, and explain what had happened. Mr.Lord then said that the award had been made to me on the grounds of my being a married man with two children, and that, should the Church in effect try to claim this to supplement their own resources, it would be withdrawn. I can still see the smile on Fr.Rees' face as he relayed this information to Canon Schofield on the telephone, and as a consequence I had a letter by return from him cancelling previous instructions! It was a relief and my initial feelings of disgust and devastation subsided, but it did leave me wondering at the apparent lack of sensitivity on the part of those who were supposed to be caring in their approach to others! This, together with a general lack of encouragement, was something that I was to experience, not just during my training, but also during my ministry as well; but more about that later.

We were further blessed at St.Michael's, with three other members of staff, all of whom made a real and lasting impression on me, and no doubt many other students as well. The first was Rev.John Cledan Mears, College Chaplain and Lecturer in Doctrine, who later became Lord Bishop of Bangor. A kindly man who loved to share knowledge; a man of deep insight regarding the needs of each student, a lover of Wales and of the native tongue, and on the lighter side, a lover also of burnt toast! He had a good sense of humour, he needed one with our year especially, but he saw us safely home in what, for all of us, was a very difficult subject.

The Rev.Elwyn Roberts, Librarian, Lecturer in Old Testament Studies and later Archdeacon of Bangor, was a very quiet and sincere man, and a gifted communicator. His lectures were full of little anecdotes for illustrations, all of which enabled us to both enjoy and retain what he had to say. He had a lovely sense of humour that he always managed to link in with his subject, even if, on the face of it, there was no apparent connection. For example, one evening, whilst he was out, we moved his bed from his bedroom, to the lecture room. The next morning during breakfast, we asked if he had enjoyed a good night. "Yes thank you", came the reply, "although this morning, as I got out of bed, I knew how the Psalmist felt when he wrote in Psalm 31, verse 8. 'Thou hast set my feet in a large room'"(Book of Common Prayer). Is it any wonder that he was held in such high esteem, and is still remembered with such affection?

The fourth member of the resident staff was the Rev Herbert Lewis Clarke, Sub-Warden, Lecturer in New Testament Studies and later Archdeacon of Llandaff; a very likeable and effervescent man who had a firm grasp on his subject, along with a firm belief in it. Because of his quickness of speech, it was initially difficult to keep pace with him, but this was helped by the fact that he handed out first class notes for our information and future reference, and as a result, one was able to feel more relaxed and therefore more able to sit back and enjoy the experience! At that time Fr and Mrs Clarke had a baby son, Christopher, and, as a married man with two children, I was asked from time to time to baby-sit for them. On one occasion, as it was nearing the time for examinations, I took with me my own New Testament shorthand notes complete with aids to memory. " Nobby", as he was always known, asked if he could see them, and appeared very intrigued to see how at least one of the 'senior' students had coped in summarizing all he had been taught in short sentences and key words, which in themselves contained the seeds for development and adaptation. He appeared well satisfied, although well aware that ultimately the proof of the pudding would be in the eating. Over thirty five years later, I still have the lecture notes he gave us, and now that he has passed into, what an old vicar of mine always referred to as, 'the kindlier world', they form a very real part of my memories of him and my gratitude for all his unstinting help, understanding and patience.

Although there are many other things I could mention about my time in St.Michael's, suffice it at this point of time, to mention one experience that I will never forget. In our second year, it was decided by 'the powers that be', that we should carry out a "Mission to Merthyr"- Merthyr Tydfil that is- the original idea being that all our year should go there for a full week, during which we would visit homes, attend parish functions, and on the Sunday assist with services and preach at them. Subsequently, for reasons I cannot now recall, this was changed and instead we were to go there in pairs over a number of weekends. Again we were to visit families and to share with them our experiences of college life, I suppose as part of a P.R. exercise, and on Sunday to help with services so far as we could, and to preach. In our particular pairing, I was to be the preacher. I was left to prepare the sermon, with the assurance that the staff were there to offer advice if I needed it, and on the understanding that the finished article had to be submitted for approval by them before it was presented. I was able to call upon my experience as a Reader and prayerfully I began to prepare. In so doing, my thoughts were turned to the Old Testament lesson for that particular evening which told the story of Jacob's Dream, (Genesis. 28. verses 10-17.) and to the penultimate verse 16, "When Jacob awoke from his sleep, he thought, 'Surely the Lord is in this place; and I was not aware of it". I chose this as my text and eventually everything was prepared, and approved with little or no modification, and now it was a matter of waiting patiently for our turn to arrive. As if this wasn't bad enough, there was worse to come as the events of the week leading up to our visit unfolded, and only two days before we were due to go to Merthyr, came news of the Aberfan Disaster, with the tragic loss of so many innocent lives. It was a terrible shock to everyone, but it was decided that our visit should go ahead as arranged. Aberfan is only, as it were, a stone's-throw from Merthyr, and in the packed congregation at evensong on the Sunday, there were many, who had either lost relatives themselves, or had friends or neighbours who had. It is no exaggeration to say that the atmosphere in church was 'electric'; charged with deep and mixed emotions and with many unspoken questions being asked in anger, despair and disbelief, to name but a few. As the time for the sermon drew near, I felt a real sense of inadequacy in myself, and I prayed for the help and guidance of the Holy Spirit in seeking to meet the needs of those who were hurting so much. It came in the realisation that the Holy Spirit had already led me to choose such a wonderfully fitting text and had fashioned my sermon so as to allow me to use the material in such a way that it spoke to them in their need, not least, in reassuring them of God's love and His presence with them in the darkness of their despair. It was an experience I will never forget; it taught me the importance of prayerful preparation and of complete reliance upon the Holy Spirit for guidance and inspiration. It was, in so many ways, to teach me the importance of humility, and to fashion the way forward in sermon preparation and delivery in the years to come.

College days duly completed, I was made Deacon by the then Bishop of Blackburn, the Rt. Rev. Charles Claxton on the 21st of May 1967, and licensed to serve in the Parish of St.Wilfrid, Standish, under the then Rector, Canon Charles Edward Bramley, always known as Peter; a very special man whom I will always remember with gratitude and affection. I was ordained Priest on the 9th of June of the following year, again by Bishop Claxton, assisted by the Rt.Rev.Frederick Amoore, Bishop of Bloemfontein, our link Diocese in South Africa. In both instances the Ordinations were held on Trinity Sunday. I remained Curate of Standish for five years, during which time we as a family were very happy indeed, and had it been left to me I would have stayed there permanently, such was the wonderful and loving working relationship I had with the congregation and parishioners of all denominations. But it was not to be, and on the 16th of August, 1972, I was Instituted and Inducted as the Vicar of the Parish of St.Paul, Low Moor, Clitheroe, now in the Ribble Valley on the borders of Lancashire and Yorkshire. Originally, Low Moor had developed as housing for the operatives of, what was then, the biggest cotton mill in the north of England. It was built and managed by the Garnett family, who also provided the bulk of the money for the building of St.Paul's Church, the Benefice of which they were also the Patrons. Because of the nature of the origin of the village, its inhabitants were a mixed group even in my incumbency there, and because they came from different communities, places and backgrounds there were occasions when we had clashes of opinion, but generally speaking we got along very well. This was helped by the fact that shortly after I arrived, the village became a grant area for modernisation, such that most of the houses were involved, and all concerned needed to become interdependent. It was a good time to get to know each other, and certainly it was a good time for the Church to be seen in action, in doing everything it could to help and support those in its care, and in promoting good will amongst all concerned. During my four and a half years there, congregations grew in number and the general standard of worship greatly improved; a robed choir was introduced, the organ was rebuilt, and a parish hall and community centre was built and paid for. In fact, on the surface, everything appeared to be going well, but sadly on a personal level this was not the case as I was suffering from deep depression, which resulted in fourteen E.C.T. (Electro-Convulsive Therapy) treatments in Burnley General Hospital; and then, shortly after the death of my Mother, I suffered a severe facial paralysis which later required corrective surgery. The then Bishop, the Rt. Rev.Robert Martineau, sent the Archdeacon of Blackburn to tell me that he thought it would be best if I resigned from the living and found other work in order to aid my recovery, with the proviso that when I was better I could return to the full-time ministry. It was at this point that I had yet another experience of the so called caring attitude of the Church, or should we say the lack of it, for not only did the Archdeacon hand over the task of conveying the Bishop's message to my wife, he didn't even bother to come upstairs to see me before he left! Nor were there any questions asked by the Diocese as to how or where, we were going to live. I left in the middle of December 1976 and I was paid up until the end of the month and that was it, except that I was given permission to officiate; but again, no reference was made or advice given as to the form any future ministry of mine might take; instead, I was left very much to plough a lone furrow. It was all very disappointing, but at the same time it provided a great deal of food for thought, in underlining the importance of that love, care and concern for people in need, which should always be of top priority in ministry. Sadly, I had not found this to be the case in the way I had been treated by the powers that be, but in no way was I going to allow this to undermine what I believed to be true and had practised in my own ministry from the very beginning, and indeed still do.

At the time I left Low Moor, jobs were not easily come by, but I was very fortunate in having as a parishioner, one of the shift managers at Messrs Whitbread's brewery which is situated at Samlesbury, Nr.Preston. I went to talk to him and explained the situation, whereupon he obtained for me an application form, which I duly completed, had an interview, and in mid January 1977, began work in one of three Bright Beer areas and, in time, became departmental training officer and Health and Safety representative for all the Bright Beer areas. I stayed at the brewery until May 1985, when, yet again, I was retired on health grounds, this time with Occupational Asthma and Acute Obstructive Airways Disease. This coincided with my wife's retirement, also on health grounds, from Messrs.Asda at Clayton Green, midway between Walton-le-Dale and Chorley. She was suffering, as indeed she still continues to do, from Emphysema, which in the course of time has become chronic and now requires full time oxygen therapy. From 1982 to 1985 I also served as a relief chaplain in H.M.P. Wymott, as and when my shift patterns at the brewery allowed; which was not only rich and valuable experience of how the other half live, but also helped a great deal financially in enabling us to pay off our outstanding mortgage when we had to retire simultaneously. From 1986 to 1988, I was an Assistant Chaplain in Sharoe Green Hospital in Preston, mainly in the Gynaecological Ward, but also to some geriatric patients as well. Again, a very interesting experience in busy wards and with many differing emotions and problems to be ministered to; with many interesting characters to provide food for thought and to challenge one's outlook on life and death. Since 1988, I have been Honorary Chaplain to St.Catherine's Hospice, Lostock Hall, Nr.Preston, which I suppose could be the subject of a further book in itself, but more of that later. From 1989 to 1992 I also assisted with services, as a yearly visitor, in St.George's Church on the military base of H.M.Forces, (Dhekelia), Cyprus, which enabled me to experience life and ministry from a very different angle in what might be termed 'the extended community'. It was also during this period, that I was privileged to meet the then Bishop in Cyprus and the Gulf, the Rt.Rev. John Brown, a very loving, kind and compassionate man who would always be my choice, although I know he would not agree, as the perfect 'Father in God'; the letters he wrote to us when we were having family problems, being reminders to us of this special man, who, together with Rosemary his wife, was 'there for us' in our time of need, and we are pleased and privileged to have them both as friends. Since 1997 I have been Honorary Assistant Priest at St.Leonard's Church, Walton-le Dale, and the Church of St.Leonard-the-Less, Samlesbury. So it would appear that the circle is nearing completion, or is it? Only time will tell and we can only deal with it thus far.

At the beginning of this chapter we found the character Jean Valjean asking WHO AM I? and in the succeeding pages I have in effect told you WHO I AM; but I hope in such a way, that in turn you will be encouraged to take a good long hard look at your own life as well. It will bring back a lot of memories, as it has for me; all of them are very precious and meaningful in our journey of discovery, or is it rediscovery? What really matters is that we look back in a prayerful and expectant way, asking that God will open our eyes to the wonders of life, our life, and enable us to see Him at work, guiding, correcting and reassuring us, whether it be at special moments in our lives, or whether it be through the influence of others working for Him. We will then be enabled to move on from explaining 'WHO I AM' to asking 'WHO AM I'? in the overall scheme of things; and to do so with the assurance that the One who has brought us thus far, will be with us every step of the way.

Let me close by sharing with you some very special words I came across attributed to Frederich Buechner, although sadly I do not know the original work from which they are taken.

Listen to your life.
See it for the fathomless mystery that it is,
in the boredom and pain of it no less than the excitement and
gladness; touch, taste, smell your way to the holy and hidden
heart of it, because in the last analysis, all moments are key
moments and life itself is grace.

CHAPTER TWO

Having previously told you about the circumstances surrounding my birth and how, had I not cried at what was a crucial moment, there is a distinct probability that I would not have survived; and having made the observation that although at the time I heard my mother telling someone about what happened I didn't know it, but obviously God had other plans for me; I have to tell you that the early years of my life hardly bore evidence of this. Some of my earliest memories are of the times I spent in Pendlebury Children's Hospital, and I distinctly remember the occasion when together with a little boy called John, I was taken to a service in the hospital chapel. Outside the window was a flagpole with its flag waving merrily in the breeze, and being so young and unable to understand what was going on in the service, quite naturally the flag held our attention, so much so that when, quite suddenly, it began to descend, John and I began to giggle and then to laugh uncontrollably, so much so that we had to be removed! When I began attending day school, there was the occasion when the Headmaster, Mr.F.E.Brewer, or "Ferdie" as he was always known by the scholars, summoned my big brother Harry and sent him down to the infants class to sort me out, because in his words I was behaving like a raging and bellowing bull! Indeed, it would appear that throughout my childhood I had the reputation for being noisy, disruptive and nearly always in mischief and trouble of one kind or another. I know that my mother, bless her, who because of my having had corrective surgery was always very protective of me, and repeatedly pleaded with me to stay out of trouble to avoid the need for more, must have despaired, and on more than one occasion I was marched along to the police station - by previous appointment of course - for a dressing down by the 'village bobby', of whom, as children, we lived in awe. Then again, one Sunday morning in Church, a group of us were in trouble for writing and drawing inside the covers of the hymn and prayer books; whilst on another occasion when we had a visiting preacher, the Reverend Canon Povey, I was in trouble again, this time for talking throughout the sermon; such that when he left the pulpit, the preacher did not return to his stall, but came down to the back of church where I was sitting, summoned a Churchwarden and I was taken home in disgrace! I don't need to tell you what this meant in terms of punishment in addition to having to make a public apology to all concerned; all of which should have taught me a lesson, but not so, as not long afterwards I was caught riding my bicycle in church, again with painful consequences. I have also mentioned earlier about my misbehaviour in Sunday School, which, on several occasions, caused my future wife Audrey to complain to her parents about me and there were no doubt others who were doing the same; so that, all in all, I think you will agree that future prospects at this stage of the proceedings were rather bleak indeed. But all was not lost, there was a glimmer of light at the end of the tunnel that came as the result of a chance Sunday evening visit to the market square in Preston, where for the first time I stopped to listen to the words of the Reverend Fred Wilson, then Minister of Carey Street Baptist Church, during one of his regular open air meetings which were always well attended. I would have been twelve or thirteen years old at the time, but I have never forgotten the feeling of warmth and well-being within me and surrounding me, as he spoke about Jesus and all He did for us on Calvary long ago and how He loves us now and longs for us to give our lives to Him and to His service. It was not something new that I had never heard before; it was the way in which I was hearing it now, for it was not just the message contained in and coming from the well worn Bible held in his hand, it was also the message which was enshrined in, and coming from his heart, which made it so precious, fresh, and so much different. Consequently it was the first of many visits to listen to this lovely man, for not only was I thrilled by the message he gave us, but also filled with a desire and longing to stand where he was standing, and to do what he was doing, a desire and a longing which, through the years and all the changing scenes of life, has now become a living reality and just as much a part of my life as everyone I have met, every place I have visited, and everything I have experienced thus far. Furthermore, although I appreciate there will be many in this world who will not agree, for me, the Holy Bible, the Word of God, is so precious; it is the manual for life, for living and for healing. It is to be read, cherished and shared; which is why it has such a major part to play in this book, as I seek to share with you the many thoughts it has provoked in me over the years, and still does day by day.

There is no doubt that the first few days, even weeks, of my two years in India were a shock to the system, for not only had I to cope with a whole new way of life and living, but also with the food, the heat and particularly the high humidity in that part of the world, and the associated problems of prickly heat and tummy upsets, not to mention the ants (in the sugar basin and everywhere else} and cockroaches, mosquitoes and lizards, but also in learning to cope with the sights, the sounds and the smells: the pavement dwellers, who are born, live and die by the side of the road, the poverty and wealth often in close proximity and yet oblivious to each other, and the beggars more often than not carrying children in various stages of disability or blindness, and others, adults and children, suffering from leprosy: the crowded streets and bazaars with the shouts of the street traders selling their wares, the noise from motor car and taxi horns and the incessant blare of the music from a multitude of sources: dogs, cows, goats and other animals roaming freely and scavenging for food: massive well loaded carts being pulled along by heavily perspiring men or by bullocks with ribs almost protruding through the skin, and womenfolk, often heavily pregnant, carrying water pots or loads of bricks, stones or wood on their heads, in the main purely by balance or perhaps with the help of one hand, whilst the other was occupied in supporting a small child being carried on one hip; and all this against a background of a cacophony of sound and colourful intermingling movement. Away from the City centre, on the seaward side of the four miles long Marina Drive, itself situated alongside the lovely beach overlooking the Bay of Bengal, were two statues, the first, at the San Tome (St.Thomas) Roman Catholic Cathedral end was of Mahatma Gandhi, portraying him as being much healthier than in real life; so much so, that the first time I saw it, there was a man alongside it fasting to death in protest! The second statue half way along the Marina featured a small group of men moving a giant boulder using wooden poles, aptly titled 'The Triumph of Labour.' On the opposite and inland side of the Marina stood the very impressive Government of Madras buildings, together with some of those of the University; a far cry, you may be thinking, from the poverty and squalor to be found in and around the city; but behind the impressive façade it was another story, for there was the 'Sweet-water Canal', which although very impressive and photogenic smelled no better than an open sewer, and certainly left one, not only with a lasting and burning impression, but also a timely reminder of the need for those in charge to get their priorities in order.

In so highly a populated city, one was not only brought face to face with the extremes of life, but also with the presence of death as well, in witnessing daily the funeral processions for all age groups ranging from premature babies to the elderly and aged. This was made even more evident by the fact that the road out of the city to the factory at Ennore passed by the burning grounds where all cremations took place, and because the dead were always visible, whether on dishes in the case of premature or tiny babies, stretchers in the case of young children, or open coffins, even carts where the deceased were seated upright on top in chairs, in the case of adults; death was being seen as just as much a part of life as being born. Yes, initially it was a shock, and although the element of shock did subside with the passage of time, for me the whole experience was precious and invaluable in preparing me for my future ministry.

There was always a choice of ways to take within the city limits, and there were many days when the journey to work took us by way of a small whitewashed church; it had no outstanding features from an architectural point of view for Prince Charles to enthuse about; in fact it was little more than a square box with a small steeple at one end, and yet for me it was very special. The attraction was not the form of the building, but a small notice in the window above the main door facing on to the street; written in English it said simply 'Come apart and rest awhile'; very inviting words indeed for those passing by in the heat and burden of the day, and in a city of three million inhabitants there was no shortage of them. But then again, these were no isolated words of invitation to passers by, or to those who, in the words of the late Noel Coward, like 'mad dogs and Englishmen, go out in the mid-day sun'; they were, and indeed still are, echoing the words of Jesus to His disciples in every generation, in the hustle and bustle of their everyday world. For as St.Mark tells us in his Gospel, there were so many people coming and going that Jesus and His disciples didn't even have chance to eat; so He said to them, "come with me by yourselves to a quiet place and get some rest" (chapter 6, verse 31); and this wonderful invitation to be quiet and alone with Him is so precious, as we seek, like Jean Valjean, to answer the question 'WHO AM I' and discover for ourselves, in so far as we are able, or in so far as we wish, whichever may be the case, God's will for us in the world and in the overall scheme of things. In so doing, I am very conscious that all of us will be at different stages and that it would be impossible to deal with every aspect, point of view or question that could possibly arise in a general approach; which is why I have chosen, for better or for worse, to proceed from the position I know best, my own experience, in the sincere hope that in some way it will speak to each of you at whatever stage on the road to heaven you may be, even searching to make a start, and to do so with the prayer that all that has gone before, and all that follows, will open the door to healing, faith, peace and fulfilment for all concerned.

My own faith is simple, I believe that Almighty God in His love created the world, and, in turn, through our parents, gave life to each and every one of us, and that when our lifespan here on earth comes to an end, be it through natural causes, accident or disasters of one kind or another, God, in His love and compassion, will receive that life back to Himself. I further believe, that whilst we are here on earth, providing we are mentally able, we are given many opportunities to know Him, to love Him, and to serve Him, without any violation of the gift of freewill He has bestowed upon us all, and that the response we make will very much influence our eternal destiny as we shall see in due course. How, then, has God given us these opportunities to know Him? He shows us His love and handiwork in the wonders of the universe and of nature; as the writer of the Book of Psalms underlines so beautifully in Psalm 19 verses 1-2, " The heavens declare the glory of God; the skies proclaim the work of his hands. Day after day they pour forth speech; night after night they display knowledge." But how can this be, when in verse 3 he writes, "They have no speech, there are no words; no sound is heard from them." In other words, they cannot speak, but yet, as the psalmist goes on to write in verse 4, "Their voice goes out into all the earth, their words to the ends of the earth." The answer is that their witness is a silent and powerful witness; they speak through what they are, rather than in what they say; but at the same time, the wonder of it all is taken up and offered on the altar of man's worship and praise throughout the world, "Come, let us sing for joy to the Lord; let us shout aloud to the Rock of our salvation. Let us come before him with thanksgiving and extol him with music and song. For the Lord is the great God, the great King above all gods. In his hand are the depths of the earth, and the mountain peaks belong to him. The sea is his, for he made it, and his hands formed the dry land. Come, let us bow down in worship, let us kneel before the Lord our Maker; for he is our God and we are the people of his pasture, the flock under his care" (Psalm 95, verses 1-7). Furthermore, one cannot think about space travel and exploration and all that they have revealed about our world, the universe, and the solar system, without the feeling of awe and reverence for their creator and ours; indeed if we were to search through the many hymn books compiled over the years, it would no doubt be possible to find many examples in support of such feelings; but perhaps none better than the following which we tend to think of as one of our modern hymns, but which has now been translated into English over fifty years and whose origin goes back further still. My, how time flies!

O Lord my God! When I in awesome wonder
Consider all the works Thy hand hath made,
I see the stars, I hear the mighty thunder,
Thy power throughout the universe displayed;
Then sings my soul, my Saviour God, to Thee,
How great Thou art! How great Thou art!
Then sings my soul, my Saviour God, to Thee,
How great Thou art! How great Thou art!

When through the woods and forest glades I wander
And hear the birds sing sweetly in the trees;
When I look down from lofty mountain grandeur,
And hear the brook, and feel the gentle breeze;
Then sings my soul, my Saviour God, to Thee,
How great Thou art! How great Thou art!
Then sings my soul, my Saviour God, to Thee,
How great Thou art! How great Thou art!

(From Hymn 506 in Complete Mission Praise, translated from Russian circa
1953 by Stuart. K. Hine)

Nor must we forget how God reveals Himself to us in the times and the seasons, and through all the changing scenes of life; a fact that inspired the author of the book Genesis to write in Chapter 8 verse 22, "As long as the earth endures, seedtime and harvest, cold and heat, summer and winter, day and night will never cease." And again, we find the author of the Book Ecclesiastes similarly inspired to write in Chapter 3 verses 1- 8, "There is a time for everything, and a season for every activity under heaven: a time to be born and a time to die, a time to plant and a time to uproot, a time to kill and a time to heal, a time to tear down and a time to build, a time to weep and a time to laugh, a time to mourn and a time to dance, a time to scatter stones and a time to gather them, a time to embrace and a time to refrain, a time to search and a time to give up, a time to keep and a time to throw away; a time to tear and a time to mend, a time to be silent and a time to speak, a time to love and a time to hate, a time for war, and a time for peace."

We are also privileged to see God at work in the lives of other people, not only in the words and examples of those who have led saintly lives, but also in the words and example of those who have influenced our lives, and made us what we are at this moment of time; parents, teachers, clergy, colleagues and friends. Nor must we for one moment forget the wonder of God's handiwork in creating us, each in a most wonderful and unique way, as advances in Genetic Engineering have begun, and will continue, to unravel, whilst the biology of the human body is a miracle in itself, from the moment of conception to the moment when this earthly life ceases to be. In Genesis Chapter1verse 26, we read, "And God said, let us make man in our image, in our likeness", and the more we study and think about what makes us tick, the more surely we need to care for God's creation, in ourselves just as much as in the world at large; an intimacy and need taken up by the Psalmist, when, in Psalm 139 verses 13 - 18, he writes "For you created my inmost being; you knit me together in my mother's womb. I praise you because I am fearfully and wonderfully made; your works are wonderful, I know that full well. My frame was not hidden from you when I was made in the secret place. When I was woven together in the depths of the earth, your eyes saw my unformed body. All the days ordained for me were written in your book before one of them came to be. How precious to me are your thoughts O God! How vast is the sum of them! Were I to count them, they would outnumber the grains of sand. When I awake, I am still with you."

But having given the above examples; inspiring though they are, we can never see God, and God at work, in a more real way than in the life and ministry of His only Son Jesus Christ, Who, in the words of the Church's Creed, "For us and for our salvation came down from heaven, was incarnate (made flesh) from the Holy Spirit and the Virgin Mary and was made man. For our sake He was crucified under Pontius Pilate; He suffered death and was buried. On the third day he rose again in accordance with the scriptures; He ascended into heaven and is seated at the right hand of the Father"; a truth taken up by the writer of the Epistle (letter) the Hebrews in Chapter 1 verses 1-3, "In the past God spoke to our forefathers at many times and in various ways, but in these last days He has spoken to us by His Son, whom He appointed heir of all things, and through whom He made the universe. (hence the plural in let us make man in our own image, after our likeness) The Son is the radiance of God's glory and the exact representation of His being, sustaining all things by His powerful word. After He had provided purification for sins, He sat down at the right hand of the Majesty in heaven." All of which, not only provides us with much food for thought, as we will go on to see, but also underlines for us in a nutshell how God also speaks to us in the inspired and inspiring words of Holy Scripture, and ultimately in the Word made flesh, His Son Jesus Christ. So often we can read the Bible and sing hymns without really thinking about the words, which is why I want us to continue thinking about the basic matters of the Christian Faith with the support of Holy Scripture and the truths that hymns convey, as they have been revealed to me over the years. I find them exciting; I hope you will too!

To begin with, we have to move into a new dimension, because we have to ask ourselves why it was so necessary for God to send Jesus into the world. There will be many who would say that Jesus came into the world to show us what God is like, and how much He loves us and cares for us, and that His miracles of healing the sick and feeding the multitudes are practical demonstrations of that love and care. They would also say that by His teaching and example, Jesus gave us the ideal pattern for human life and behaviour, in loving God with all our heart, mind, soul and strength, and our neighbour as ourselves, and certainly all of this is true, but it is not the full story.

To put it in a nutshell, Jesus came into the world as God's answer, and the only solution, to the deepest needs of sinful mankind. The Bible is only one chapter old when, in chapters 2 & 3 of the Book Genesis, we have the story of the Garden of Eden, the Garden of God's presence, where Adam and Eve are told that they may eat the fruit of all the trees in the garden, except the fruit of the tree of the knowledge of good and evil, for if they do, they will surely die; the choice is theirs. Now comes temptation in the form of the serpent; very slippery, subtle and crafty in his move on Eve, for when she tells him what God has told them about what they can and should not do, he responds by saying, don't worry, you won't die; the reason God has warned you off the tree of the knowledge of good and evil is because He knows that then you will be as wise as He is. "When the woman saw that the fruit of the tree was good for food, and pleasing to the eye, and also desirable for gaining wisdom, (chapter 3 verse 6) she took some and ate it. She also gave some to her husband who was with her, and he ate it."

Verses 7 - 24 then go on to tell us how, immediately, their eyes were opened and they realised they were naked; in other words, they realised that the choice they had made was flawed; they felt exposed, the peace they had known in God's presence was no longer there, and although they tried hard to cover their nakedness, they could not, and when God called to them, they hid themselves from Him amongst the trees of the garden. When God then challenged Adam to face up to the truth of the error of his ways, what happened, he blamed God! - "The woman you gave to be with me, she gave me of the fruit of the tree and I ate it"; nor is Eve when challenged, willing to take the blame -"the serpent beguiled me"! So, the serpent was condemned by God to live on its belly and to eat of the dust of the ground all the days of its life, and furthermore was told "I will put enmity between you and the woman, and between your offspring and hers; he will crush your head, and you will strike his heel;" a matter to which I will return later. Eve, for her part, is told, "I will greatly increase your pains in childbearing; with pain you will give birth to children, and yet, your desire will be for your husband, and he will rule over you." Adam also receives his comeuppance, "Cursed is the ground because of you; through painful toil you will eat of it all the days of your life. It will produce thorns and thistles for you, and you will eat the plants of the field. By the sweat of your brow you will eat your food until you return to the ground, since from it you are taken; for dust you are and to dust you will return."

So we see that the story of Eden, besides being one of disobedience and its consequences for those concerned, is also one of the breakdown of relationships between God and man, man and his fellow man, and man and the world of nature; and the story closes with Adam and Eve being expelled from the garden, for the Lord God said "The man has now become like one of us, knowing good and evil. He must not be allowed to reach out his hand and take also from the tree of life and eat, and live for ever." At first sight this appears a very harsh and unforgiving thing for God to do, but had He not done so, and they had then eaten of the tree of life in their state of alienation from God, there would have been no way back, nor would this book have been written; it was in fact God's first loving and forgiving move in His plan for healing the rift, and providing the only way to restore mankind to the Garden of His Presence, in and through His only Son, "that whoever believes in Him shall not perish but have eternal life. For God did not send His Son into the world to condemn the world, but to save the world through Him."(John chapter 3 verses 16-17) Furthermore, in John's First Letter, chapter 5 verses 11-12, he gives further qualification to that contained in his Gospel above, namely, "And this is the testimony: God has given us eternal life, and this life is in His Son. He who has the Son has life; he who does not have the Son of God does not have life." In other words, God's free gift of eternal life, although offered to all, will only become a reality for those who believe and trust in

His Son Jesus Christ and accept Him into their hearts and lives as Lord and Saviour; for in so doing they move from being children of God in general - for it is from God that all life comes into being- to become children of God in particular, or, as the phrase in the Book of Common Prayer Baptism Service has it, they become members of Christ, children of God, and inheritors of the Kingdom of Heaven.

It is at this point that I wish to qualify something that I said earlier in this chapter about mental ability and our being able to deal with the opportunities which God gives us to know, love, and serve Him, without any violation of the gift of freewill He has given to us all; and particularly so when, as we have seen, the response we make will very much influence our eternal destiny. It is my belief that those who, through severe mental handicap, even though they are not precluded from experiencing the loving presence of God in their lives, are unable to make this response for themselves are in no danger, in that by the same token, they are unable to exercise freewill and therefore by God's love and mercy, in and through the Sacrament of Holy Baptism and with the prayerful support of family and friends, they are assured of heaven.

For the rest of us however, it is a different story, and the choice has to be made one way or the other; one of the biggest problems being that for the majority this is not readily recognised. People in general do not see that there is a problem; they see heaven as the place they can enter under their own steam, by living a good life and by helping others all they can; both of which are very admirable and desirable qualities which God would like to see in all of us, but which do not deal with the heart of the problem, namely that of Sin and its inevitable consequences. For as St.Paul tells us in Chapter 6 verse 23 of his Letter to the Romans, "the wages of sin is death, but the gift of God is eternal life in Christ Jesus our Lord." It therefore follows, that because we are the descendants of Adam, although in our moment of birth we have committed no sin, yet we still share in his sin of disobedience and in the inevitable consequence of it, death. So that we are in a position which, of ourselves, we can do absolutely nothing about; there is no way that any amount of Do It Yourself can provide a solution; only God in His love and mercy could do that, which He did in sending Jesus into the world to die for us on Calvary; for as that lovely hymn 'There is a green hill far away' by Mrs. C.F.Alexander (1818-95), expresses so beautifully,

We may not know, we cannot tell,
What pains He had to bear,
But we believe it was for us
He hung and suffered there.

He died that we might be forgiven,
He died to make us good;
That we might go at last to heaven,
Saved by His precious blood.

There was no other good enough
To pay the price of sin;
He only could unlock the gate
Of heaven, and let us in.

I have faithfully copied these words as they are in the hymn book, but I never read or sing them without wishing that Mrs Alexander had changed the punctuation in the last two lines of the final verse above to read,

He only, could unlock the gate
Of heaven and let us in.

For I feel sure that this is what she wanted to say, and especially when she has already said in the opening lines of the verse,

There was no other good enough
To pay the price of sin

It may be that it had something to do with the meter of the verse, or to suit the tune that was subsequently added, who knows; suffice it to say that in the end Jesus alone, could, and did open the kingdom of heaven to all who believe and trust in Him; but what was the thinking behind this?

In the Letter to the Hebrews chapter 9 verse 22, we read, "the law (Jewish law that is) requires that nearly everything be cleansed with blood, and without the shedding of blood there is no forgiveness." Consequently, if the situation resulting from the sin and disobedience of mankind, together with its inevitable consequences, was to be remedied, then two conditions had to

be fulfilled. Firstly, it must involve the outpouring of blood in sacrifice, and
secondly, the sacrifice had to be offered by one who was sinless. In the Old
Testament, it was the blood of animals that was offered daily in the temple
by the priests on behalf of those who sought forgiveness, but on the Day
of Atonement, (Yom Kippur) it was the High Priest alone who entered the
Holy of Holies, the Most Holy Place in the temple, again with the blood of
animals, to make reparation for the nation. But first he had to make reparation
for himself and his own sins. All of which meant that God's plan for the
redemption of the world could never be fulfilled under the old covenant, the
old way of doing things, but rather under a new and living way, through Jesus
the Great High Priest, Who, Himself sinless, entered into the Holy of Holies,
not of the temple, but of Heaven, into the Eternal Presence of God, carrying,
not the blood of bulls and goats, but His own blood, poured out on the Cross
of Calvary for the sins of the whole world, for your sins and mine.

> And when I think that God His Son not sparing,
> Sent Him to die - I scarce can take it in.
> That on the cross my burden gladly bearing,
> He bled and died to take away my sin.
> Then sings my soul, my Saviour God, to Thee,
> How great Thou art! How great Thou art!
> Then sings my soul, my Saviour God, to Thee,
> How great Thou art! How great Thou art!

(From hymn 506 Complete Mission Praise, referred to earlier)

It is at this point that we need to clarify the sinless-ness of Jesus. In the
Church's Creed we are reminded that it was, for us and for our salvation
He came down from heaven, was incarnate from the Holy Spirit and the
Virgin Mary and was made man; and that means fully man, for as we read in
Hebrews chapter 4 verse 15, "we do not have a high priest who is unable to
sympathise with our weaknesses, but we have one who has been tempted in
every way, just as we are - yet was without sin." In other words it was not that
Jesus was unable to sin, otherwise He would have been less than fully man,
but rather that He was able not to sin.

Earlier, when dealing with the disobedience of Adam and Eve in the Garden
of Eden, I said that we would return to think further about the words of God

to the serpent, namely, "I will put enmity between you and the woman, and between your offspring and hers; he will crush your head, and you will strike his heel." Here I believe we have a prophecy in the form of a veiled reference to the perfect offering made by Jesus on the Cross of Calvary. For it was on the cross that Jesus crushed the serpent's head in winning the ultimate victory over sin and death, thus robbing the tempter of his power; but in so doing the serpent struck His heel, and it cost Jesus His life. It is also interesting at this point to note the reversal of what happened in the Garden of Eden with all that happened in the Garden of Gethsemane and later on Golgotha, the place of the skull, or Calvary as we know it. In Eden, we see the disobedience of Adam and Eve; in Gethsemane the perfect obedience of Jesus whose birth was made possible by the perfect obedience of His Mother Mary, who, in the documents of the early church is referred to as 'The Second Eve'. In Eden, the Tree of Life in the midst of the garden, was scorned by Adam and Eve in favour of the Tree of the knowledge of good and evil, which in turn became for them the tree of death; in Gethsemane we see in the acceptance by Jesus of His Father's will, His embracing of the Cross which the Jews always thought of as a curse, for as the Book Deuteronomy has it in chapter 21 verse 23 said "anyone who is hung on a tree is under God's curse"; while on Calvary the tree of death became the Tree of Life.

When I survey the wondrous cross
On which the Prince of glory died
My richest gains I count but loss,
And pour contempt on all my pride.

Forbid it, Lord, that I should boast,
Save in the death of Christ my God;
All the vain things that charm me most,
I sacrifice them to His blood.

See from His head, His Hands, His feet,
Sorrow and love flow mingled down;
Did e'er such love and sorrow meet,
Or thorns compose so rich a crown?

> Were the whole realm of nature mine,
> That were an offering far too small,
> Love so amazing, so divine,
> Demands my soul, my life, my all.

Words by Isaac Watts, 1674-1748.

So then, the facts of the case are clear; through the disobedience of Adam and Eve the whole of mankind is tainted and destined to die in sin and only God in His love and mercy could remedy the situation, and this He did in and through the death and resurrection of His only Son Jesus Christ, in what the Prayer of Consecration in the Holy Communion Service of 1662 states as "a full, perfect, and sufficient sacrifice, oblation and satisfaction for the sins of the whole world"; a very profound statement which means that the perfect sacrifice made by Jesus on the Cross was complete and cannot be repeated, and that by it God was completely satisfied in that the price of sin had been paid in full by the Sinless One, His beloved Son. A thought taken up by St.Paul in his first letter to the Corinthians chapter 15 verses 21-22,

"For since death came through a man, the resurrection of the dead comes also through a man. For as in Adam all die, so in Christ all will be made alive

And again in his letter to the Romans chapter 6 verses 9-11 we read,

"For we know that since Christ was raised from the dead, he cannot die again; death no longer has mastery over him. The death he died, he died to sin once for all; but the life he lives, he lives to God. In the same way, count yourselves dead to sin but alive to God in Christ Jesus."

What we are seeing here is the demonstration of a fundamental truth, namely, that the Christian Faith is not a way of life as many believe it to be, but is belief in a person, Jesus Christ, who stands at the very heart of God's plan on Salvation for the world. To be 'In Christ', one of St'Paul's favourite sayings, is to trust Him with our very lives, all we have been, all that we are, and all that we have the potential to become, in the sure knowledge that we have the promise and blessed assurance of sins forgiven and eternal life restored, whereas without Christ we have no such assurance, and consequently it is a frightening thought, that the choice we all have to make is no less than a choice between life and death. On the face of it there would appear to be no problem, in that to choose life would seem to be the most obvious and desirable thing to do; but that being the case then, why is it that so many people decide otherwise; why do so many still treat Jesus as an optional extra they can accept or reject at will to suit their circumstances at the time? Then again, what about those who have felt the need to accept Jesus into their hearts and lives and yet go on delaying to do anything about it, leaving it to another time, another day; a very dangerous game to play, because as experiences in life have a habit of showing us, there may not be another time or another day. They need to heed the advice of the Psalmist in Psalm 95 verse 8,

"Today, if you hear his voice, do not harden your hearts."

This is underlining the sense of urgency in a matter that not only has its implications for physical death and beyond, but also for the here and now as well, as St.Paul says in his second letter to the Corinthians, chapter 5 verse 17, "Therefore, if anyone is in Christ, he is a new creation; the old has gone, the new has come!" But again, we must ask why, in the face of so much promise and assurance, so many still decide otherwise; could it be that they would like the gifts that life in Jesus brings, but without the commitment, service and sacrifice that being "In Christ" also entails; but which, when undertaken in love for Him and in thanksgiving for all that He has done for us, can take on a new and joyous perspective and a deep fulfilment, in being privileged to undertake something really worthwhile in sharing in God's plan for the salvation of the world with others. This is something we will return to later when we turn our thoughts to discipleship and all this means for us in our world today; suffice it to say that whilst it may not be the only reason why people decide not to respond to Christ, it would seem that the point we have made in this paragraph demands attention.

From early New Testament times-and we must remember, if we had not realised it already, that the Epistles of St.Paul for example were written before the Four Gospels of Matthew, Mark, Luke and John - to become "In Christ", or to undergo Christian Initiation, has been through Baptism, which means washing with water: sometimes as individuals, sometimes as whole families or households, and usually by total immersion as was the case with our Lord's own Baptism by John the Baptist in the River Jordan. But this means more than ritual washing or cleansing, although the latter is a very important feature, as St Paul in his Letter to the Romans, chapter 6 verses 3-6 makes clear, "Don't you know that all of us who were baptised into Christ Jesus were baptised into his death? We were therefore buried with him through baptism into death (underwater) in order that, just as Christ was raised from the dead through the glory of the Father, we too may live a new life. If we have been united with him like this in his death, we will certainly be also united with him in his resurrection. For we know our old self was crucified with him so that the body of sin might be done away with, that we should no longer be slaves to sin."

In Baptism, a brand new living relationship with God is formed in, and through, the death and resurrection of Jesus; which in effect goes back to the dawn of time and onwards into eternity; a thought that is underlined in some words by the poet Hartley Coleridge in his sonnet, 'The Just shall live by Faith'

Think not that the faith by which the just shall live,
Is a dead creed, a map correct of heaven?
Far less a feeling fond and fugitive,
a thoughtless gift withdrawn as soon as given
is an affirmation and an act, which bids eternal truth be present fact.

"An affirmation and an act,"- a decision to be made by the individual, to turn to Christ, to repent of their sins, and to renounce evil. Or, to put it another way, to turn one's back upon the devil and the darkness of this world and to turn instead to Jesus the Light of the World, into whose hands we give our life for all time and for all eternity.

I am trusting Thee, Lord Jesus,
Trusting only Thee;
Trusting Thee for full salvation,
Great and free.

I am trusting Thee for pardon,
At Thy feet I bow;
For Thy grace and tender mercy,
Trusting now.

I am trusting Thee for cleansing,
In the crimson flood;
Trusting Thee to make me holy,
By Thy blood.

I am trusting Thee to guide me;
Thou alone shalt lead,
Every day and hour supplying
All my need.

I am trusting Thee for power,
Thine can never fail;
Words which Thou Thyself shalt give me
Must prevail.

I am trusting Thee Lord Jesus;
Never let me fall;
I am trusting Thee for ever,
And for all.

Frances Ridley Havergal 1836-79

These words are an expression of the writers search for, and dedication to, the One who stands at the very heart of the matter, Jesus Christ, and a desire to trust Him forever and for all things needful. They may well have come into being as the result of some experience or even crisis in the author's life, which made her realise that she could no longer cope with life under her own steam; that she desperately needed the help that only Jesus could give her and which in turn necessitated her giving of herself to Him. Consequently, we see all of this reflected in the above hymn and in another of her well known and much loved hymns,

Take my life, and let it be
Consecrated, Lord, to Thee;
Take my moments and my days,
Let them flow in ceaseless praise.

Take my hands, and let them move
At the impulse of Thy love;
Take my feet, and let them be
Swift and beautiful for Thee.

Take my voice, and let me sing
Always, only, for my King;
Take my lips, and let them be
Filled with messages from Thee.

Take my silver and my gold,
Not a mite would I withhold;
Take my intellect, and use
Every power as Thou shalt choose.

Take my will, and make it Thine;
It shall be no longer mine:
Take my heart, it is Thine own;
It shall be Thy royal throne.

Take my love; my Lord, I pour
At Thy feet its treasure store;
Take myself, and I will be
Ever, only, all, for Thee.

It would be very interesting indeed to know what reactions we have to reading the words of these two hymns. Do they sum up how we feel, do we really relate to what they have to say, do they give us a feeling of warmth and well-being deep down inside, such that we could very happily add our own Amen to them? Or, on the other hand, do they fill us with an overwhelming wish that we could make for ourselves a similar commitment to that being made by the author of them? These are very searching questions, the answers to which will have a great deal to say about our own personal faith and the stage we have reached in our spiritual pilgrimage.

There is also no doubt, from my own experience and the experience of many others, that the deeper the sense of personal sin and the need for help is, the deeper the sense of need to be 'in Christ' becomes; resulting for many, in them taking the necessary steps to remedy the situation in and through Holy Baptism and all that it implies in repentance for past sins, by a conscious about turn from the darkness of the world to Jesus the Light of the World, and by a personal renunciation of evil; of the devil and all his works. But what about those of us who were Baptised as babies or young children and as such were incapable of making such acts of repentance and renunciation and of turning to Christ for ourselves, but were dependant on our God-parents doing this on our behalf? And even though in the course of time, many of us went on to Confirm these for ourselves, in general it was at a time in our lives when emotions and hormones are confused, such that although we may remember well the occasion, it is doubtful whether we fully appreciated what was really happening, even though those who prepared us had done their very best to enlighten us.

Consequently, there is a real sense in which, although our Baptism is valid and we are 'in Christ', we can still feel a deep need to go on confirming our faith in Jesus as we grow in grace and mature both in our thinking and in our Christian Discipleship; and as we come to realise more and more the gifts of the Holy Spirit, which in Confirmation were bestowed upon us, the Spirit of wisdom and understanding; the Spirit of counsel and inward strength; the Spirit of knowledge and true godliness; that we may rejoice in the understanding and ways of the Lord.

In addition to what has gone before, there is also the desperate need for us to persist in our striving against evil in its many forms, not only in our world, but also in our lives. For while it is true that through His death on the cross, Jesus won the ultimate victory over sin and death such that they can have no eternal significance, the devil is still a real force to be reckoned with in this life. Which is why we need the help and guidance of the Holy Spirit in searching the Word of God in Holy Scripture.

In his first letter, St John writes, "If we claim to be without sin, we deceive ourselves and the truth is not in us. If we confess our sins, he is faithful and just and will forgive us our sins and purify us from all unrighteousness." (Chapter 1 verses 8 and 9); and in St.Luke's Gospel chapter 15 verses 18-19, we have the words of the Prodigal Son which in so many ways reflect the problem we all face at sometime or another, "I will set out and go back to my father and will say to him: Father, I have sinned against heaven and against you. I am no longer worthy to be called your son; make me like one of your hired men," whilst in St. Paul's letter to the Romans, considered by many to be his personal testimony, we hear him struggling with sin in his life in a way that has a great deal to say to us in our struggles as well. From the pen of the greatest ambassador for Christ the world has ever known, we have his frank admission of the terrible dilemma he finds himself in, and from which he finds himself completely powerless to escape; so let us see what he has to say, and the solution he has found to his deepest need and ours, in chapter 7 verses 18 - 25.

"I know that nothing good lives in me, that is, in my sinful nature. For I have the desire to do what is good, but I cannot carry it out. For what I do is not the good I want to do; no, the evil I do not want to do - this I keep on doing. Now if I do what I do not want to do, it is no longer I who do it, but it is the sin living in me that does it So I find this law at work: When I want to do good, evil is right there with me. For in my inner being I delight in God's law; but I see another law at work in the members of my body, waging war against the law of my mind and making me a prisoner of the law of sin at work within my members. What a wretched man I am! Who will rescue me from this body of death? Thanks be to God - through Jesus Christ our Lord!" Yes, I know this is a difficult passage and we may need to read it several times before the truth of it sinks in, even though in a very real sense it is only seeking to express in words what many of us will have experienced in our own lives; furthermore, our understanding of Paul's mind in this respect will also be helped, if we go on to read three sections of chapter 8 of this same Letter to the Romans.

"Therefore, there is now no condemnation for those who are in Christ Jesus, because through Christ Jesus the law of the Spirit of life set me free from the law of sin and death. For what the law was powerless to do in that it was weakened by the sinful nature, God did by sending his own Son in the likeness of sinful man to be a sin offering. And so he condemned sin in sinful man, in order that the righteous requirements of the law might be fully met in us, who do not live according to the sinful nature but according to the Spirit. Those who live according to the sinful nature have their minds set on what that nature desires; but those who live in accordance with the Spirit have their minds set on what the Spirit desires." (verses 1-5)

"Those controlled by the sinful nature cannot please God. You, however, are controlled not by the sinful nature but by the Spirit, if the Spirit of God lives in you. And if anyone does not have the Spirit of Christ, he does not belong to Christ. But if Christ is in you, your body is dead because of sin, yet your spirit is alive because of righteousness. And if the Spirit of him who raised Jesus from the dead is living in you, he who raised Christ from the dead will also give life to your mortal bodies through his Spirit, who lives in you." (verses 8-11)

"For if you live according to the sinful nature, you will die; but if by the Spirit you put to death the misdeeds of the body, you will live, because those who are led by the Spirit of God are sons of God. For you did not receive a spirit that makes you a slave again to fear, but you received the Spirit of sonship. And by him we cry, "Abba, Father." The Spirit himself testifies with our spirit that we are God's children. Now if we are children, then we are heirs - heirs of God and co-heirs with Christ, if indeed we share in his sufferings in order that we may also share in his glory." (verses 13-17)

Here again, it may take several readings of the above verses before we fully grasp them, - it certainly did in my case - but it is all worthwhile in that it enables us to see into Paul's mind and, as we said earlier, to understand his dilemma and its solution to be found in Jesus Christ and God's precious gift of eternal life to all who believe and trust in Him. We also see the conflict in his mind as he battles with the power of sin, which he still sees as a force to be reckoned with in his life, and as such, finds it extremely difficult and well nigh impossible to live a life in keeping with this blessed assurance. It requires serious and spirited effort at all times; a fact he recommends to his readers in his first letter to the Corinthians chapter 9 verses 24 - 27,

"Do you not know that in a race all the runners run, but only one gets the prize? Run in such a way as to get the prize. Everyone who competes in the games goes into strict training. They do it to get a crown that will not last; but we do it to get a crown that will last forever. Therefore I do not run like a man running aimlessly; I do not fight like a man beating the air. No, I beat my body and make it my slave, so that after I have preached to others, I myself will not be disqualified for the prize."

Such is the translation in the New International Version, but having been nurtured on the King James Version, I always feel that the latter expresses Paul's dilemma and deep seated concern much better in a final verse which reads, "But I keep under my body, and bring it into subjection; lest that by any means, when I have preached to others, I myself should be a castaway." Maybe, this appeals to me because it is a concern very near to my own heart, in that so often in preaching to others one can so easily lose sight of one's own shortcomings and the need to strive afresh against the foe every day.

Almost at the beginning of this chapter, I explained that, because all of us are at different stages in our spiritual progress, and because it would be impossible to deal with every aspect that could arise, I had chosen, for better or for worse, to proceed from the point of view I know best, my own, and it is to this end I now return in seeking to bring it to a close.

As I look back, I am very conscious indeed of the effects of the power of evil in my life thus far, and of the many times, when, in thought word and deed, I have sinned against Almighty God, our Heavenly Father, and my neighbour, through negligence, through weakness and through my own deliberate fault; and it makes me so sad to think of the unnecessary pain I have caused to His Heart and the hearts of others, all of whom were quite undeserving of it, and for which I am more profoundly sorry than words can ever express. Like St.Paul I am also aware that the battle is far from over, and that the need to fight against evil is an ever present need; like him I am very much aware of the fact that in my own strength I am helpless to cope and that the dilemma he experienced in his life, and which we have looked at in detail, is so much mirrored in mine. Like Paul, I am filled with adoration, with love, and with loving gratitude, for the love of God, Whose readiness to forgive us our sins, to restore us to grace and to give us His precious free gift of eternal life in and through His beloved Son, our Lord and Saviour Jesus Christ, is a continuous cause for thanksgiving and the best possible incentive I can ever have for a daily renewal of my belief, faith, and trust, in Him. So that my faith in Jesus is that living faith, which in the words of Hartley Coleridge already quoted previously, " bids eternal truth be present fact"; a daily walk with Him, sharing each day with Him, asking for His help and guidance, and for His strength to face everything the day brings, come what may, that His will, and not mine, may be done, and so that the harvest in His Name and to His glory may be great. And though there will be many times in the days ahead when I will fall short of what He would have me be and do for Him, I have the blessed assurance of sins forgiven for every truly penitent heart, and the comforting thought that, although in Jesus every saint may have a past, so also, in Him, every sinner has a future! It is as a sinner who has experienced for himself, forgiveness through the Cleansing Blood of Jesus, and who now stands continuously in the need of grace, that I dedicate my life anew, day by day, to Him and to His service in the world, that I may be a living channel for His healing and peace, and so that I may share with others, what Jesus means, and has done, for me, and will do for them and for everyone who will give

Him the opportunity. This is my reason for living and for this book! May it help you to discover your faith in a new and living way, and how you too can find fulfilment in life and realise your own truly God-given potential, in a life of loving service for Him in the world.

WHO AM I then, in the overall scheme of things? Through the love, mercy and forgiveness of Almighty God, I am His (in loving obedience and service) and He is mine (not to own, but as my Rock through all the changing scenes and storms of life and forever): and it can be the same for you as well because this is God's free gift to all who believe and trust in His Son Jesus Christ as their Lord and Saviour for all time and for all Eternity.

Two prayers for everyday -

Thank you Lord,
> for your precious gift to us of life,

Thank you Lord,
> for your precious free gift of eternal life, in and through
> your beloved Son, our Lord and Saviour Jesus Christ,

Thank you Lord,
> for your precious gift of your Most Holy Spirit, to be the
> Lord and giver of life to the Church; to lead us into all
> truth, and to help us to grow into the fullness of the
> stature of your dear Son,

Thank you Lord,
> for everything. Amen.

Alan Hunt

Lord Jesus,
I give you my life,

Take it,
Break it,
Make it,
Fill it with your light,

So may I serve others,
And be faithful to the end.

Amen.

(From an ordination card sent to me; origin unknown)

Postscript

About the year 2000 I was in a shop in Preston waiting to be served. The elderly gentleman in front of me, whose face I could not see, was buying vitamin pills; I know this because he was asking the assistant serving him for advice. In her reply she referred to him by name, Reverend Wilson! My heart missed a beat! Could it be the man who had inspired me so much so many years ago? Yes it was, and as he walked very slowly from the shop I followed him and called his name. He turned and when he saw me he asked if he should know me. It was then that I told him what had happened long ago and all that had happened since. As I did so, his eyes filled with tears and so did mine, and he said simply "Praise the Lord!" I'm so glad I had the opportunity to tell him, because not long afterwards he passed into the 'kindlier world', and it was right for him to know how his ministry had been blessed yet again.

CHAPTER THREE

There is a saying that Christianity is caught and not taught; and whilst we may or may not agree with this sentiment, I think we can say that there are certainly elements of truth in it, and that we have practical examples of these in what I have told you about my visits to the market square in Preston to listen to the Rev. Fred Wilson, and also in the inspiration I have also received from the various personalities who have figured prominently in my life since, some of whom I have already mentioned and others who are still to come. But this is only part of the picture, for all of these lovely people, who, in many and various ways have helped to make me what I am now, have in fact been the messengers and the channels, leading me to the very heart of the matter, to Jesus Himself; to discover some of the many things that combined to make Him so special, and which were the keys to His undoubted success whilst here on earth.

In St.John's Gospel, chapter 12 verses 32-33, Jesus says, "I, when I am lifted up from the earth, will draw all men to myself"; and John goes on to add his own observation, "He said this to show the kind of death He was going to die." But is that the whole story, or was there some deeper reason behind the words of Jesus, and does it provide the key to His success that we are looking for? My reason for asking this is because in St.John chapter 10 verses 14-16, we have some further words of Jesus that are very interesting, when He says, "I am the good shepherd; I know my sheep and my sheep know me - just as the Father knows me and I know the Father - and I lay down my life for the sheep. I have other sheep that are not of this sheep pen. I must bring them also. They too will listen to my voice, and there shall be one flock and one shepherd."

Dr.William Barclay, in commenting on these words from John chapter 10 in 'The Daily Study Bible', has something very interesting to say, namely, "Jesus describes Himself as the good shepherd. Now, in Greek, there are two words for good. There is the word agathos which simply describes the moral quality of a thing; there is also the word kalos which means that a thing or a person is not only good; but in the goodness there is a quality of winsomeness, loveliness, attractiveness which makes it a lovely thing. Now, when Jesus is described as the good shepherd, the word is kalos. In Jesus there is more than efficiency, and more than fidelity; there is a certain loveliness."

Loveliness, winsomeness and attractiveness: all of which combined in the magnetism of Jesus. I am the good shepherd; I am the attractive shepherd; I am the magnetic shepherd. So much so, that when we think about our Lord's own ministry as a whole, we cannot help but realise that it was His attractiveness, His magnetism, which was one of the key factors in its success. Otherwise we would find it very difficult indeed to understand how a simple carpenter from Nazareth was so successful, not only in His calling and leadership of a small group of disciples, made up of fishermen, a tax collector, a zealot or two and other occupations and backgrounds, but also in His being able to communicate freely with young and old alike from all walks of life. For while it is true that not all of them responded to His challenge in the way He would have liked, there can be no doubt that Jesus got through to them in such a way that they may not have been able to put into words but certainly could not deny. His magnetic personality, His perceptiveness, His deep love and concern for God's children and creation and many other factors, all combine to give Him that completeness which lies before us all as the perfect example for which those who are called to be His disciples must be striving continually; in the knowledge that the One who calls them to be with Him before sending them out in His Name, will, through the power of the Holy Spirit, inspire their minds, inflame their hearts and strengthen their wills, that they may know more clearly the Gospel, the Good News of Jesus and so be enabled to communicate it more fully to others in His Name and for His sake.

Here and now, as of old, we have the invitation of the One whose disciples we are called to be, to "come apart and rest awhile" and to be able, in the face of the changes and chances of this world, with all its complications, frustrations and needs, to sit at the feet of the One Who never changes, Who is the same yesterday, today and forever; there to find anew from the Master what discipleship and ministry are all about, and how they involve our whole being and the need for our constant vigilance and effort. "I sign you with the sign of the cross to show that you must not be ashamed to confess the faith of Christ crucified, and manfully to fight under His banner against sin, the world and the devil, and to continue Christ's faithful soldier and servant unto your life's end." (Holy Baptism - Book of Common Prayer)

Dr. Barclay concludes his observations on the section referred to above by saying, "In the picture of Jesus as the Good Shepherd there is loveliness as well as strength and power. In the parable the flock is the Church of Christ. And the flock suffers from a double danger. It is always liable to attack from outside from the wolves and the robbers and the marauders. It is always liable to attack from the inside from the false shepherd. The Church runs a double danger. It is always under attack from outside. It often suffers from the tragedy of bad leadership, from the disaster of shepherds who see their calling as a career and not as a means of service. The second is by far the worse; because, if the shepherd is faithful and good, there is a strong defence from the attack from the outside; but if the shepherd is faithless and a hireling, then the foes from outside can penetrate into and destroy the flock. The Church's first essential is a leadership which is based on the example of Jesus Christ"

Here is a great deal of food for thought for us all, clergy and laity alike, as it is very easy at this point to be critical of those in either group whom we consider to have fallen short of the high standard set by the Good Shepherd; whereas it would be good for us instead, to think about how those high standards were reflected practically in His life and ministry, so that we may have a more balanced and informed view on which to develop a more positive and constructive opinion.

One of the outstanding features of the public ministry of Jesus was that He was always accessible to those in need, whether it be in hunger, in poverty, in sickness or in sin. He made no reservations, His invitation was to all, high or low, rich or poor, Pharisee or publican, Scribe or sinner, loved one or leper; the outward trappings did not matter, Jesus did not make fish of one and fowl of another. He was more concerned to meet the need within, whatever that need might be; all that He asked was that they should come to Him;

"Come to me, all you who are weary and burdened, and I will give
you rest. Take my yoke upon you and learn from me, for I am
gentle and humble in heart, and you will find rest for your souls.
For my yoke is easy and my burden is light."

(St.Matthew. chapter 11 verses 28-30)

and always with this invitation came the Blessed assurance;

"All that the Father gives me will come to me, and whoever comes
to me I will never drive away."

(St.John, chapter 6 verse 37)

53

Nor was His invitation conditional upon convenience. We do not get the impression from the Gospels that His willingness to help depended on whether or not He had time, for with the exception of those few times when He went apart to be quiet, to pray and to commune with His Father, Jesus always had time, be it day or night, to meet the needs of those who came to Him, as, when, or where they arose. There are two instances which come immediately to mind; the first being His first miracle at the wedding at Cana of Galilee, when in answer to an embarrassing emergency He turned water into the best wine they had ever tasted, (St John's Gospel chapter 2 verses 1-11); and the second His healing of the woman who had suffered for years from a severe haemorrhage, and who came and touched the hem of His garment in the middle of a crowd. (St.Matthew's Gospel, chapter 9 verses 20-26, and St.Mark's Gospel, chapter 5 verses 24-34.) Nor did Jesus consider the narrow confines of the Jewish Sabbath as in any way a barrier when need arose, and He readily made His feelings known to those who did, (St.Luke's Gospel, chapter 14 verses 1-6). We could say that the concern of Jesus to meet need in these and many other ways was motivated purely by love and compassion; but the more I think about it, the more convinced I become that there were other factors involved, not least His home life with Mary and Joseph and His work as a carpenter in the village of Nazareth.

Although from the Gospels we have only an outline of those early years, mainly from the Gospel of St.Luke, chapter 2, we are given the impression that against the background of a simple and loving home, Jesus was raised in the Jewish faith and all that it required. From early days He would be taught to say His prayers and later to learn passages of Scripture off by heart, even before he was able to read them. When He was twelve years of age, like all Jewish boys, He celebrated His 'Bar Mitzvah', His becoming a 'Son of the Law', and could then take His place amongst the men in the synagogue, and receive training, not only to read properly, but also to read the Sacred Scriptures publicly. It was also at that special time in his life, that He referred to God as His Father as St.Luke records for us in chapter 2 verse 49; "Why were you searching for me?" He asked Mary and Joseph, who had been searching for Him anxiously for three days before finding Him in the temple courts, sitting among the teachers, listening to them and asking them questions to the amazement of all concerned. "Didn't you know I had to be in my Father's house?" But even so, this did not alter His relationship with Mary and Joseph, He still remained the loving and obedient Son and He continued to grow both in body and in wisdom, gaining favour with God and men, (St.Luke chapter 2 verses 51-52).

Then again, although the Gospels have nothing to say on the matter, a further eighteen years passed from His 'Bar-Mitzvah', before His public ministry began. These again were precious years, when Jesus served His apprenticeship with Joseph to become a carpenter, much of which would again be caught and not taught, to become a skilled craftsman in His own right; so that when Joseph eventually died, Jesus not only undertook responsibility for the family business, but also the family itself. This He was well equipped to do because He had served His apprenticeship not only to His trade, but also to life, and there is no substitute for shop-floor experience! Throughout those years Jesus gained rich experience, not only in the art of woodworking, but also in dealing with the many problems of home and business life, and with the personal relationships which emerged from both; along with the extra demands which being a servant to the community resulted in. So that in a very real sense, there was a rich tapestry woven into the life of Jesus prior to the commencement of His public ministry, which very much fashioned His character, His attitude and His ability to communicate with others, which together with His love for His Father and for all God's children, meant that He was ideally prepared for the ministry to come.

In his book 'Testament of Faith' already referred to, Dr, William Barclay writes, "It has been well said that there are two kinds of education, one teaches us how to make a living and the other teaches us how to live," and in the life of Jesus, we not only find the perfect combination of both, but also a very real pointer to the fact that preparation for discipleship and ministry must also contain both elements as it did for the Master Himself. Sadly this has been one matter which seemingly has been overlooked by those responsible for the selection and training of candidates for the Church's Ministry in the past; where far too much emphasis has been placed on obtaining university degrees and far too little on obtaining experience in the University of Life. To some extent this has also led to the acceptance of many, who, although academically brilliant, have eventually proved hopelessly ineffective, when it comes to dealing with people and their problems. It has also resulted, in far too many instances, in the Sacred Ministry being seen as a career which one chooses to follow, rather than being chosen to follow, again with often disastrous results, not least in those in need having little or no access to many clergy outside 'working hours' or set 'surgery times'; a situation far removed from the loving accessibility of Jesus at all times without thought of convenience.

In the Finale of 'Les Misērables'- the Musical - three of the characters, Valjean, Fantine and Eponine sing these words, "Take my hand and lead me to salvation. Take my love, for love is everlasting, and remember the truth that once was spoken, to love another person is to see the face of God." In my opinion, here, in a nutshell, we see the basic requirements for all who are called to ministry and discipleship; above all, they are to be based upon and inspired by love; love for God, love for Jesus, and, in keeping with the thinking of St Paul in his letter to the Romans chapter 14 verse 15, the brother (or sister) for whom Christ died. It involves more than a cosmetic, take it or leave it kind of love portrayed by both the Priest and the Levite in the Parable of the Good Samaritan, who, upon seeing the plight of the one who had been attacked and his need for assistance, allowed their duties in the temple to take priority over that need, and so passed by on the other side of the road. Rather, it means being a people-person, ready and willing to reach out in love to take the hand of the one in need, remembering that Jesus has no hands but our hands, no feet but our feet, no voice but our voice and that, in whatever situation of need we find ourselves, we are there for Him, and under His guidance and protection. It isn't a case of making the best of a bad job, or of thinking of other jobs we could or should be doing because we think they come higher on our list of priorities; it is as if, at this moment of time there is no other job in the world, and as such it demands our complete and undivided attention, without thought of time or convenience or possible consequences, because we are doing it for Jesus, it is His will and the outcome is therefore in His hands as indeed we are too. It is as if He says to us, 'don't be anxious, don't be afraid, remember I am with you always; reach out in love, my love, to those who need to know so much my saving ways and that my love for you and for them is everlasting; and you will experience in your life, in a deeper and more real way than ever before, the presence and countenance of God.'

Such then, is the challenge and the promise of the King of Love; the basic requirements and ground-rules for all of us, clergy and laity alike, who are called to ministry and discipleship in His Name and for His sake in the world, and we must bear them very much in mind as we go on to think about the more practical implications of this precious partnership with Him, in which we are privileged to share. We must also bear in mind that the Church as a whole is not to be thought of in terms of being a pond to fish in; as merely the place to circulate and exchange ideas and to plan strategies; all of which is positive and necessary, but which can also lead, if we are not careful, to stagnation. Rather we must see the Church not as a pond to fish in, but as a boat to fish from; in faith and in eager anticipation of a great catch for the One who says to us as He said to His first disciples long ago, "Follow me and I will make you fishers of men" (St.Mark's Gospel, chapter 1 verse 17).

When Jesus calls to discipleship, it is a two-fold calling; in the first place to follow Him, and then, secondly, through following Him to be made by Him into fishers of men, not so that like fish they might die; but rather, that by being caught in the net of God's love, they might be given eternal life. And although times may have changed from the tranquillity of the Galilean lakeside to the hustle and bustle of the twenty-first century, this fundamental condition of discipleship has not changed one iota, and does have a great deal to say to us as we in turn respond to the Master's call.

In the first place, this calling to be fishers of men would seem to imply that discipleship will only be really effective through those who have been called by Jesus and have made a positive response to His call; preferably by acknowledging Him as their personal Lord and Saviour and by committing their lives to Him and to His service. But this is not to say that there are no other levels of service that are acceptable to Jesus and commended by Him. We find evidence of this in St.Mark's Gospel chapter 9 verses 38-41, where John says "Teacher, we saw a man who was driving out demons in your name and we told him to stop, because he was not one of us." "Do not stop him," Jesus said, "No-one who does a miracle in my name can in the next moment say anything bad about me, for whoever is not against us is for us. I assure you that anyone who gives you a cup of water because you belong to Christ will certainly not lose his reward."

Secondly, the initial call to discipleship is to be seen in a very personal way; it is in the first place a call to follow Jesus, regardless of those previously called to join the 'team' and by the same token, those who will join it after us. In other words, it is our relationship with Jesus that must take priority over all other relationships within the team. We see this underlined in St.John's Gospel, chapter 21, verses 20-22, "Peter turned and saw that the disciple whom Jesus loved was following them. (This was the one who had leaned back against Jesus at the supper and had said, 'Lord, who is going to betray you?') When Peter saw him, he asked, 'Lord, what about him?' Jesus answered, 'If I want him to remain alive until I return, what is that to you? You must follow me.'"

Thirdly, Jesus in his call to discipleship was at pains to deal with the problems of ambition and jealousy within the 'team' and to make sure that members of it were fully aware of the ultimate aim of those called; namely to lives dedicated to the service of others. All of which is clearly seen in St.Matthew's account of the incident where the mother of James and John came to Jesus to ask that her two sons might be given the places of honour at His right hand and at His left when He became king. When the other ten disciples heard about this, they became angry with the two brothers and so Jesus called them all together and said, "you know that the rulers of the heathen have power over them and the leaders have complete authority. This, however, is not the way it shall be among you. Instead, whoever wants to become great among you must be your servant, and whoever wants to be first must be your slave - just as the Son of Man did not come to be served, but to serve, and to give his life as a ransom for many" (Chapter 20,verses 20-28). Furthermore, it is interesting to note that when St Mark records this same incident in chapter 10, verses 35 - 45 of his Gospel, it is the two disciples themselves who approach Jesus, and not their mother Salome. In other words then, the call to become a disciple, a fisher of men, is a call to become the servant of all; for just as God has reconciled us to Himself by Jesus Christ and has given us the ministry of reconciliation, (2 Corinthians chapter 5, verse 18) so we also are to see ourselves within this work as labourers together with God (1 Corinthians chapter 3, verse 9); and because of this we are to seek for that humility so richly found in our Master; the humility which keeps our eyes firmly fixed on Him, so that we may not be self-seeking on the one hand or jealous of our fellow disciples on the other, but instead united in love and purpose to the furtherance of His will and His kingdom here on earth. This is why the call to discipleship is not to be thought of in terms of the promotion of denominationalism within the Christian Church, for as history has shown in no uncertain terms, the witness of the Church as a whole has been seriously hampered and weakened by its self-imposed and self-perpetuating divisions and disunity, where discipleship itself has mistakenly been seen as the promotion of the teachings and traditions of individual churches, rather than the teachings of the Master and Lord of all. Also, in many cases, the work of the Holy Spirit, so vital to the life of the Church, has been stifled, or dare we say it, ignored, and the calling of many to be fishers of men overlooked and allowed to fall through the net; resulting not only in the loss of essential man power in a time of great need, but also in unnecessary frustrations and often suffering for the individuals concerned, each of whom is precious to God and who, having been obedient to the Master's call must begin to wonder what on earth is happening, whilst some, like the rich young man in St.Matthew chapter 19.verse 22, walk away, because they consider the risk too much in the hands of those who over the years have done little to inspire confidence. Nor can we at this stage ignore the marked decrease in vocations in all denominations. Could it be the Holy Spirit's way of warning the Church of the error of her ways? We shall see. One thing, however, that cannot be denied at this point is that the Church which allows those truly called to ministry, and particularly to the Sacred Ministry, to slip through the net, is not only failing in its basic duty by denying the wish of the Master Himself, but is also doing so with the result that the discipleship of others is also seriously undermined. If the Church as a whole, is to fulfil the will of its Lord and Master, and to be a really effective missionary force in the world in its greatest hour of need, it needs desperately to put its own house in order and to seriously reconsider and revise the system of recruitment and training, so that none are precluded by virtue of social background or academic ability, but rather are allowed and encouraged to find the fulfilment of their individual potential. Only then will the Holy Spirit's guidance in so many be given free rein and be brought to fruition, and many will echo the words from the lovely hymn, 'Dear Lord and Father of Mankind' by John Greenleaf Whittier, 1807-1882.

> In simple trust like theirs who heard,
> Beside the Syrian sea,
> The gracious calling of the Lord,
> Let us, like them, without a word
> Rise up and follow Thee.

(verse 2)

When Jesus called the Twelve, made up, as mentioned at the beginning of this chapter, of fishermen, a tax collector, a zealot or two and other occupations and backgrounds, He knew there was an element of risk in all of them, because He knew that they were part of fallen humanity, just as He also knew that they possessed free-will and, that like all of us, they would increasingly become prey for the devil's temptations. In time Judas was to betray Him, Peter 'the Rock' was to deny Him, Thomas was to doubt Him, and all of them were to forsake Him at His arrest in the Garden of Gethsemane. But despite all their human faults and failings, Jesus called them, 'warts and all', and they followed Him. As a consequence, anyone called by Jesus, although conscious of their own shortcomings, can be assured of His faith in them - a faith born out of His knowledge of their hidden potential - a faith which in turn not only inspires confidence but also invites a loving and faithful response to Him in obedience, witness and service.

If the above then, represents in broad outline, not only the meaning, but also the ultimate aim and purpose of ministry and discipleship, let us turn our thoughts now to the art of fishing, in order to see how the basic requirements of 'angling' are to be applied to 'fishing for men', and also some of the many lessons the Church as a whole has to learn from them.

(a) For fishing, as for everything else, there is a time.

In the third chapter of the book Ecclesiastes verses 1-8, a passage to which we have already referred to earlier in Chapter 2, the writer explains how, as he sees it, everything that happens in this world, happens at the time in keeping with the very nature of things.

"There is a time for everything,
and a season for every activity under heaven:
a time to be born and a time to die,
a time to plant and a time to uproot,
a time to kill and a time to heal,
a time to tear down and a time to build,
a time to weep and a time to laugh,
a time to mourn and a time to dance,
a time to scatter stones and a time to gather them,
a time to embrace and a time to refrain,
a time to search and a time to give up,
a time to keep and a time to throw away,
a time to tear and a time to mend,
a time to love and a time to hate,
a time for war and a time for peace."

And this is true for fishing as it is for everything else; there is a time, there is a season, and this is also true for fishing for men, just as it is also true for those called to be fishers of men, for as Jesus says in St.John chapter 15 verse 16,

"You did not choose me, but I chose you and
appointed you to go and bear fruit, fruit that
will last."

Again, in the Book of the Acts of the Apostles, chapter 9 verses 15-17, we read how the Lord says to Ananias, "Go! This man (Saul of Tarsus) is my chosen instrument to carry my name before the Gentiles and their kings and before the people of Israel. I will show him how much he must suffer for my name." Then Ananias went to the house and entered it. Placing his hands on Saul, he said, "Brother Saul, the Lord - Jesus, who appeared to you on the road as you were coming here - has sent me so that you may see again and be filled with the Holy Spirit." For Saul of Tarsus it was time - God's time; for Ananias it was time - God's time, even though he himself was not keen to go because of Saul's reputation, (chapter 9 verse 13) and "immediately, something like scales fell from Saul's eyes, and he could see again. He got up and was baptised, and after taking some food, he regained his strength" (verses 18 and 19).

We also have, in St Paul's first letter to the Corinthians, chapter 3 verses 6-7, a real insight into team spirit with each other and with God. "I (Paul) sowed the seed, Apollos watered the plant, but God made it grow. So neither the one who sows or the one who waters is anything, but only God who makes things grow." I rather beg to think that God would not agree when Paul infers that neither he nor Apollos are important in the overall scheme of things; and Paul himself even goes on to contradict this, when in verses 8-9 he speaks of himself and others as God's fellow workers having one purpose, and each being rewarded according to his own labour.

Now, if we really think about the foregoing, we will come to see that much of the impatience and frustration which so often accompanies the consciousness of one's calling to discipleship and particularly the subsequent practical application of that calling, is not only unnecessary, but also results in a detrimental effect on our thinking and our work. For whilst is it very tempting to be impetuous in order to 'get on with things', unless the time is right, and hence the timing is right, it will bear no fruit. Instead we have to pray for patience, to wait expectantly upon God, knowing that His timing is always perfect, and in the words of St Paul to the Philippians, chapter 1 verse 6, "confident of this, that he who began a good work in you (us) will carry it on to completion until the day of Christ Jesus."(Words previously referred to earlier in this book as the text given to me, and my fellow candidates, at our Confirmation by Bishop Askwith.) But having said this, what about the occasional apparent contradictions to it; what about the man or woman, devoted to God and His work in the fullest sense of the word, at the height of their powers, doing so much good in the world, being of so much help and giving so much inspiration to so many people through their ministry, with so much to give and with so much potential still to come; and then suddenly it is not to be? Here, no doubt, the thoughts of some will turn to the late Reverend David Watson and to the shock, distress, and questions that his death from cancer on February 18th 1984, caused amongst his fellow Christians. He was known loved and respected worldwide as a gifted preacher and Christian communicator and his dynamic ministry lives on through his writing. His book, 'I believe in the Church', explores the revolutionary potential of the family of God. It draws on the years of leadership and learning at St Michael-le-Belfrey, York, (next door to the Minster) where he was Vicar. His other titles include Discipleship; I believe in Evangelism; Is there anyone there?; One in the Spirit; Through the year with David Watson; You are my God; and his final book Fear no evil, telling his personal struggle with cancer. So we begin to realise what an aching void his death caused for so many here and throughout the world, and in order to begin to understand the meaning of it all we need to hear David's own thoughts as in the penultimate page of Fear no evil, (page 171) he tells how, in his helplessness, he cried out to God to speak to him, which He did, so powerfully and painfully that David had never felt so broken before Him. "He showed me that all my preaching, writing and other ministry was absolutely nothing (in italics) compared to my love-relationship with him. In fact, my sheer busyness had squeezed out the close intimacy I had known with him during the first few months of the year after my operation." So that what David is apparently implying here is that at the end of the day, it is not the past success or future potential of his ministry and discipleship which matters, but his relationship with his Lord and Master, which is so paramount, and without which everything else in his own words was "absolutely nothing." Once this relationship had been restored nothing else mattered; David was willingly and completely in God's care and time and timing were now in His hands. "Whatever is happening to me physically, God is working deeply in my life. His challenge to me can be summed up in three words: 'Seek my face.' I am not now clinging to physical life (though I still believe that God can heal and wants to heal); but I am clinging to the Lord. I am ready to go and to be with Christ forever. That would be literally heaven. But I am equally ready to stay, if that is what God wants.

'Father, not my will but yours be done.' In that position of security I have experienced again his perfect love; a love that casts out all fear."

Those were David's final written words in the first week of January 1984 and in the Epilogue written after his death we read, "From January 16th David's condition deteriorated very rapidly. He continued to see close friends from time to time and on Monday 30th he said to David MacInnes: 'I am completely at peace - there is nothing that I want more than to go to heaven. I know how good it is.'" David lived long enough to see members of his team when they returned from five weeks ministry in California and he especially enjoyed times with his wife and children. "Late on the evening of Friday 17th February he said to his wife Anne: 'I'm very tired; let's go home.' David Watson died peacefully very early next morning.

'The Lord Reigns'"

How then, after reading all of this, can we say, as many did at the time, that David had passed into the presence of his Risen Lord and Master prematurely and with his work unfinished? Indeed, his final days and words sum up completely what waiting upon God is all about; and that when the time for, and the timing of, discipleship and ministry is completely in the hands of God, there will always be time to accomplish all that He has for us to do, and even though this may not be apparent at the time for those whom we love and to whom we minister, it will be revealed in God's own good time.

(b) In fishing for men, it is necessary to study their curious ways.

There are two well known sayings 'up North', namely 'there's nowt so queer as folk,' and 'everybody's a bit queer except me and thee, and I'm not so sure about thee.' (In both instances 'queer' having no inference to human sexuality as it does in our modern world!) Well, the dialect may change as we move from one area to another, but there is no doubt that parallels to both of these sayings will be found not only in this country but throughout the world; each underlining in its own way, the uncertainty and unpredictability to be found in individuals in the response they make to any approach made to them; which in turn will have a marked effect on the outlook and strategy of those called to ministry and discipleship. Consequently, we must never lose sight of the importance of gaining as much experience as we can of human nature and behaviour patterns; by readily accepting the experiences of everyday life and living, as a real and essential part of our preparation for ministry and discipleship. In this sense we never stop learning; there is always some new experience, ordinary and perhaps at times unpleasant or even uninteresting though it can be, or some new snippet of knowledge to be gained, all of which are important factors in our preparation, as the One who calls us to His service, leads us into these situations, so that we may learn and be equipped for that work. There is no set pattern, no set syllabus for the course, nor are there specific class times to be observed and kept, no, we are to wait on Him at all times, and to be ready to respond to His guidance through the Holy Spirit without delay, so that we and our study of the fishes' curious ways may be completely in His hands. Then, and only then, will we be able to appreciate how the apprenticeship that Jesus served before the commencement of His own public ministry, must find a realistic parallel in all those He calls to follow Him. For every one year of His ministry, ten had been spent in studying the fishes' curious ways; all of which should provide us with plenty of food for thought and be a restraining influence in our times of frustration and impatience. So that like the many occasions in the Gospels when the Master Himself said 'My hour is not yet come', we too, in waiting patiently on Him, will know the time to let down the net for the best possible results, for He knows the fishes' curious ways, He knows when the time is right.

(c) In fishing for men, we must have the right equipment, not only to catch men, but also to bring them safely to shore.

In the hymn 'Stand up! Stand up for Jesus!' we read as part of verse 3, these words, which I feel sure many of us will have sung with gusto on many occasions,

Put on the Gospel armour,
Each piece put on with prayer;
Where duty calls, or danger,
Be never wanting there

George Duffield 1818-88

These words are expressing in song, the thoughts of St.Paul, when, in his Letter to the Ephesians, Chapter 6 verses 10-18, he writes, "Finally, be strong in the Lord and in his mighty power. Put on the full armour of God so that you can take your stand against the devil's schemes. For our struggle is not against flesh and blood, but against the rulers, against the authorities, against the powers of this dark world and against spiritual forces of evil in the heavenly realms. Therefore put on the full armour of God, so that when the day of evil comes, you may be able to stand your ground, and after you have done everything to stand. Stand firm then, with the belt of truth buckled around your waist, with the breastplate of righteousness in place, and with your feet fitted with the readiness that comes from the gospel of peace. In addition to all this, take up the shield of faith, with which you can extinguish all the flaming arrows of the evil one. Take the helmet of salvation and the sword of the Spirit, which is the word of God. And pray in the Spirit on all occasions with all kinds of prayers and requests. With this in mind, be alert and always keep on praying for all the saints."

Just as the fisherman needs to have all the necessary protective clothing to cover every eventuality weather-wise, and the proper fishing tackle for the job in hand; the same is true for the fishers of men. St Paul, for his part, is in no doubt about this, for he knows that it isn't just a case of a straight forward persuasion of men, women and children to accept Jesus into their lives; he knows that the devil, for his part, will do all in his power to prevent this happening. So that there will be a constant battle to be fought against the devil and the forces of evil in the world, where the devil will use his guile and every subtle temptation in his own armoury, as he did with Adam and Eve in the Garden of Eden long ago, and has done in every generation since. As such, proper protection is of vital importance; the whole armour of God, each piece of which has a vital part to play, and which is to be put on with prayer, the precious gift of God as the lifeline to and from His presence, anywhere, any moment and of paramount importance, so that the fisher of men's equipment is right for the occasion; the rod and line strong and flexible enough, the float and hook carefully chosen and fitted, the bait fresh and inviting, and the landing net strong and in the best possible condition, lest, after careful preparation and much effort, the human fishes are allowed to slip through the net of God's love and care. Furthermore, it has to be said that whilst in all of this there are general guidelines to follow, both from our own experience thus far, if any, and from the experiences of others through the ages before us, no two instances are ever identical, because of the time and circumstances, and because of the climate, socially, nationally and worldly, any one of which can have a real effect upon the outcome, and of course because of the fishes curious ways. As a consequence we need to be fresh, alert and, as far as possible, relaxed, in our approach in order to be receptive to the guidance of the Holy Spirit, in order to be the willing channels for His transforming power in the lives of others. To this end, the preparation has to be right and it has to be prayerful; 'put on the Gospel armour, each piece put on with prayer.'

In the early days of my ministry, sermon preparation was never easy and consequently many were the times I suffered from 'Saturday nightmare,' because I had not been able to decide what to preach about, and as such, had sat for long periods staring at a blank piece of paper. What is more, even after burning the midnight oil, so often the end product had apparently made little or no impact on those who were the recipients the following day. Then came the realisation that if this situation was to be reversed, if my sermons were to be relevant, if they were to speak in a real way to the problems, difficulties and frustrations being experienced in the lives of those who had come to Church in need of help, guidance and reassurance, then the only answer must lie with the One who knows all the needs of His children, the One to Whom all hearts are open, all desires known and from Whom no secrets are hidden. Consequently, where before I had decided, often with extreme difficulty, what to preach about, it now became my practice, as indeed it still is today over forty five years later, to read through all the relevant prayers and readings for the particular Sunday or Feast day and prayerfully commit them to the Holy Spirit for His guidance. Oh yes, it still involves time and effort, not to mention with the passing of the years, difficulty often in finding the right words, but the hesitancy and the frustration are gone and as a consequence, what was once at times a chore is now a joy and a privilege with blessings for all - praise the Lord!

The same must also be true of our witness for Jesus Christ in all walks of life, for if that witness is to be timely and effective, it can only come from this same prayerful waiting upon the Lord, for as Jesus assures His Disciples of every generation; before the end comes, "the Gospel must first be preached to all nations. Whenever you are arrested and brought to trial, do not worry beforehand about what to say. Just say whatever is given you at the time, for it is not you speaking, but the Holy Spirit" (St Mark's Gospel chapter 13, verses 10-11).

(d) As fishers of men, we must always face towards the source of light.

As a young boy, one of the first lessons I was taught in fishing for 'tiddlers,' was never to let my shadow fall upon the water, in case my movements caused a distraction for the fish I was hoping to catch. So I was taught that whenever and wherever possible I should face the light; a lesson that applies just as much, if not more so, to the fisher of men as it does to the catcher of fish. For so often, if we are not careful, our own personality and will, important though they are in the process of things, can easily overshadow what we are trying to do and as a consequence what we are speaks much louder than what we say! This is why it is vitally important that in our calling to be 'fishers of men' we constantly face the one true light, Jesus the Light of the World; not only because we have in Him the perfect example we are to follow, the Master in whose steps we are to tread, but also because if we are to be 'good' fishermen, in the same sense that He was and is the Good Shepherd; if we are to be attractive, then it must be as the willing channels of the magnetism of the One Who says, " I, if I be lifted up, will draw all men unto me" (St. John's Gospel, chapter 12, verse 32). Here again is a gentle reminder that while we may take, as we must, every care in our preparation, in having the right equipment, in our study of the fish's curious ways and in our learning from the experiences of others in the past; the fact remains that the whole situation and its potential harvest, is known only to Jesus, and as such we need to be completely open and receptive to His guidance, through the Holy Spirit, and obedient to His will at all times.

To be a fisher of men is not easy, and often difficult lessons have to be learned; on occasions things we are asked and guided to do may seem illogical, just as there will be times when, like those first disciples of His, we too will be tempted to say," but Master we have toiled all night and taken nothing". It may be inconvenient, we may be very busy mending the nets and doing what we feel is essential maintenance work; but when the order comes to "launch out into the deep and let down your net for a catch", our response must be immediate and without question, whatever time of day or night. It is then that we too will experience the wonder of what can and will be achieved when His will and not ours is done; and even if in our joy we are brought to our knees as Peter, the 'Big Fisherman' was to his, when on the Sea of Galilee he saw the size of the catch he never expected or thought possible because his own efforts had proved fruitless, realised and recognised his own 'littleness of faith' and said, "depart from me for I am a sinful man O Lord" (St.Luke's Gospel, chapter 5, verse 8); then so be it, it is a lesson we all need to learn.

Having begun this chapter with the saying that Christianity is caught and not taught; a generalisation rather than a specific trend, and having dealt in turn with some, not all, aspects of discipleship, we need to draw together the various demands which this work lays upon those who undertake it and set alongside these, the fact that Jesus calls us as we are 'warts and all'. We come as individuals, created in God's image and possessing the personality together with gifts and talents we have received from Him; and while there is no doubt that so very often the raw material needs to be knocked into shape and the rough edges removed through prayer and forgiveness, individuality remains and is vitally important, otherwise much of the loveliness, winsomeness and attractiveness, all of which combined in the magnetism of Jesus, and which need to be reflected in the lives of His disciples, would be lost, with the result that outreach and mission would become stereotyped and lose much of its appeal. The ideal is seen when the individuality reflects personal acceptance of, and commitment to, Jesus, as Saviour and Friend: such that those who see this faith and commitment in action and how much it means to us will want to share and embrace it for themselves.

Furthermore we also have to appreciate that for many, the individuality of which we have spoken, will also have to be seen against the background of membership of the Christian Family, the Family of God, the Church; such that we have as it were three strands, first the overall missionary activity and outreach of the Church, second, the Church's teaching, preaching and propagation of the Gospel, the Good News of our Lord Jesus Christ, and third, the witness of individuals like us in the ordinary and everyday situations into which we are led, and enabled in the power of the Holy Spirit to share the Good News with others.

There are, no doubt, many and various ways of dealing with these aspects and the number of books already written in this respect are legion. Suffice it for our purposes to keep it, so far as is possible, plain and simple, and to deal with them under three headings of a prayer, a hymn, and a song, bearing in mind the words of St Augustine of Hippo, when he wrote, "He who sings prays twice"!

Jesus came into the world to be the Saviour of the world, and it is His will and His commission to His disciples and followers in every generation, to make Him known; to lift Him up to the whole world. Consequently, it is incumbent upon us, not only to pray for ourselves, that we may be faithful in fulfilling our Christian calling and commission, but also for each other, that together our witness may be united and fruitful, in the power of the Holy Spirit, through our Lord Jesus Christ to the praise and glory of God our Heavenly Father. To this end, I feel the simple and uncomplicated Mission Prayer chosen by the Diocese of Blackburn for the 'Call to Mission', circa 1968, is ideal.

> Come, Holy Spirit of God,
> To inspire our minds,
> Inflame our hearts and strengthen our wills,
> That we may know more clearly the Gospel of Salvation,
> And show it forth more fully to others,
> For Jesus Christ's sake.
>
> Amen.

The Church's teaching, preaching and propagation of the Gospel, the Good News of Jesus, is perhaps best summed up in the words of a friend of mine for many years, Rev Canon Edward. J. Burns, in his lovely hymn, 'We have a Gospel to Proclaim'.

> WE have a gospel to proclaim,
> Good news for men in all the earth,
> The gospel of a Saviour's name:
> We sing his glory, tell his worth.
>
> Tell of his birth at Bethlehem,
> Not in a royal house or hall,

But in a stable dark and dim:
The Word made flesh, a light for all.

Tell of his death at Calvary,
Hated by those he came to save,
In lonely suffering on the cross:
For all he loved, his life he gave.

Tell of that glorious Easter morn,
Empty the tomb, for he was free:
He broke the power of death and hell
That we might share his victory.

Tell of his reign at God's right hand,
By all creation glorified;
He sends his Spirit on his Church,
To live for him, the Lamb who died.

Now we rejoice to name him King:
Jesus is Lord of all the earth.
This gospel message we proclaim;
We sing his glory, tell his worth.

When it comes to the individual witness of ordinary folks like you and me in the world, I have thought long and hard, and searched high and low for what I consider to be a fitting example from the world today of what is a most precious privilege; and again I found it in the words of a very good friend of mine, the International Singer and Songwriter Mr.Charlie Landsborough, in his song 'My Forever Friend'. It isn't very easy to witness for Jesus on stage, and over the years Charlie has been criticised by fellow artists and others in show business for this, but remains resolute and never misses an opportunity to stand up and be counted amongst those who love the Lord! I will let his words speak for themselves because I am sure that when you have read them, you too will understand why I chose them.

Everybody needs a little help sometime,
No one stands alone,
Makes no difference if you're just a child like me,
Or a king upon a throne,
For there are no exceptions, we all stand in the line,
Everybody needs a friend,
Let me tell you of mine.

He's my Forever Friend,
My leave-me never friend,
From darkest night to rainbow's end,
He's my Forever Friend.

Even when I turn away He cares for me,
His love no one can shake,
Even as I walk away, He's by my side,
With every step I take.
And sometimes I forget Him, my halo fails to shine,
Sometimes I'm not His friend,
But He is always mine.

He's my Forever Friend,
My leave-me never friend,
From darkest night to rainbow's end,
He's my Forever Friend.

If you still don't know the one I'm talking of
I think it's time you knew,
Long ago, and far away, upon a cross,
My friend died for you,
So if you'd like to meet Him, and don't know what to do,
Ask my friend into your heart and He'll be your friend too.

He's my Forever Friend,
My leave-me never friend,
From darkest night to rainbow's end,
He's my Forever Friend.

PS. In concert this song always carries the dedication "To my Saviour, Jesus Christ", and the final chorus has an additional fifth line; "JESUS, is my best friend."

CHAPTER FOUR

In the Introduction to his book 'Discipleship', first published in 1981, the late David Watson wrote these words; "The future prospects of the affluent West are now so serious that the Christian church cannot afford to ignore the plan that Jesus chose for the renewal of society. He came with no political manifesto. He rejected all thoughts of violence. He shunned all positions of influence in public life. His plan, which was to change the history of the world in a way that has never been equalled, was astonishingly simple. He drew around him a small band of dedicated disciples. For the best part of three years he lived with them, shared with them, cared for them, taught them, corrected them, trusted them, forgave them, and loved them to the end. They, on their part, sometimes failed him, hurt him, disappointed him, and sinned against him. Yet never once did he withdraw his love from them and later, empowered by the promised Holy Spirit, this group of trained disciples turned the world of their day upside down."

How then, we may ask, is the Christian Church as a whole, coping with the pressing needs of the twenty-first century AD? What positive and helpful suggestions is it putting forward to deal with the increasing problems of drug, alcohol, sex and child abuse, with the as yet unrealised consequences of the AIDS epidemic, sexual licence, promiscuity, pornography and paedophilia? Not to mention the hopelessness of unemployment and the terror which lurks in our streets to threaten young and old alike, in muggings, rape, bullying and acts of vandalism. Then there is the general disregard for law and order in rioting and hooliganism, and for human life in war and acts of international terrorism and hostage taking, to gain political prestige and advantage, while the overall threat of a nuclear holocaust is still with us, even though the 'cold war' is long ended. Present indications are that the Church is not faring too well, for in times which are crying out for leadership, reassurance and inspiration, the Church appears tongue-tied, and unable to speak out with any kind of conviction or authority; not because of lack of effort, for of reports, conferences, commissions, crusades, reunion schemes and liturgical reforms, we have ample evidence, but with no real outcome or significant contribution towards solving the present crisis. And why, because of an apparent uneasiness in upholding true Christian values, and an unwillingness to stand up and be counted on the things that really matter in life and living, which has led not only to the undermining of Christian marriage and family life but also to the manifold problems of human sexuality, to name but a few. Again, in an effort to be all things to all men, we have the all too often compromising of Christian values in a mistaken attempt to woo those who feel that the Christian Faith is too demanding, and as such would prefer a watered-down version of it; something they would steadfastly refuse to accept in their secular life and existence. All of which makes a mockery of the whole situation, where over secularisation has led to increased frustration and a serious weakening of Christian witness. Nor has the situation been helped, by the inordinate amount of time spent in underlining the complexities of denominational differences and theological disagreements; in the emphasizing of the things that separate and weaken witness, rather than in promoting with thanksgiving, our common heritage, "one Lord, one faith, one baptism, one God and Father of all, who is over all and through all and in all." (Ephesians, chapter 4 verse 5) This has resulted in the simplicity of Discipleship - the promotion of Christ's plan for the world - having to take second place to churchianity, with its emphasis on committee-ment, rather than commitment, as a luxury which it can ill afford; for while Nero was entitled to 'fiddle' all he wished as Rome burned, the Church on the other hand is under a higher authority and will have to answer for the time wasted on contemplating its own navel while the needs of the world remain unmet and its injustices and moral decline unchallenged.

For a part of the period I was working as an engineer in South India, we had as Works Manager a canny Scotsman by the name of Jim Pollock, and I will always remember him asking, at one of our production meetings, " can ye no instil a sense of urgency into these people?" In many ways it was a cry of despair, and one would think that to ask for the same sense of urgency in our religious leaders would be unnecessary, but apparently not!

In early October 1985, the late Mrs Mary Whitehouse, wrote to the then Archbishop of Canterbury, the Roman Catholic Archbishop of Westminster, the Moderator of the General Assembly of the Church of Scotland and the Moderator of the Free Church Federal Council, saying, among other things, "the roots of the calamities which are now befalling us, from Aids to child abuse, all have their origins in the destruction of personal and national character and the undermining of Christian values." She then went on to say that "it could be a wonderful stimulus to national renewal if they - to whom she was writing - were to add their voices to those of the media, the medical and social services, the law and anguished parents, who are expressing their great dismay at the present state of our country!" How true, how sad, and what a tragedy that our spiritual leaders of the time needed such an outspoken challenge to do what should have come naturally to them. How sad too, that two decades later, she would still have had reason to write a similar letter! How is it that the powers that be, appear to be so completely out of touch with the situation at grass roots? There will be some of course who will challenge such a generalisation, but at the same time many more who will support it!

When the report 'Faith in the City' was published, also in 1985, the then Bishop of Liverpool, the Rt. Rev. David Shepherd, a member of the Commission, in one of the television interviews in which he took part, said that 'the Church of England could speak with authority on the situation at grass roots because it had agents there in the person of the Vicar or Parish Priest.' Why he made the distinction between the Church of England and other denominations is not clear; unless he was thinking in terms of it being the Established Church of the land; what is clear is that having a physical presence 'on the shop floor' as it were, does not necessarily mean having one's finger on the pulse. It will all very much depend upon the personality of those on the shop floor, and their ability to communicate their findings, and the willingness of those in authority to listen and to act accordingly.

As regards the position of those on the 'front line', it has to be acknowledged that they are, as it were, under fire from two sides. On the one hand, the past twenty years or so have seen great changes in the way people live. No longer is this nation of ours the industrial giant it once was. Factory and plant closures have led to mass redundancies and re-locations with their knock-on effects to communities and to other smaller support industries; while the uncertainties of the whole economic climate here and throughout the world has tended to make people very insular and protective of the family unit, such that on modern estates, very few know who their neighbours are, and there is little or no sense of community or belonging. Meanwhile, in towns and cities, many areas have been decimated by the clearance of older property - all in the name of progress of course - with the subsequent breakdown in the kind of community life many of us experienced in our earlier days and which meant so much in making us what we are; and although the emergence of 'Neighbourhood Watch' schemes has had a real part to play in our modern society, they can only touch the surface of that mutual responsibility and interdependence which was so much a part of everyday life, in sickness and in health, and which meant so much to all concerned. Then again, the many stresses of life and living have led to family estrangements and breakdowns; there has been a great increase in those suffering from depressive and psychiatric illnesses while the instances of child abuse in the home and in the community are now, sadly, an ever present fact of life. Nor can we ignore the upsurge in cases of domestic violence in the community, not just in towns and cities, but in rural areas as well. One day on the programme Kilroy, which was dealing with this very subject, a detective inspector from Sussex, told viewers that in that county alone in 2002 there had been 15,500 reported cases, in 80% of which women were the victims, and the remaining 20% the men. If these were the reported cases, one may wonder what the true figure really was! Plus the fact that because of the general loss of community, and the insular nature of family life that has developed, so often cases of child abuse and domestic violence continue unobserved and only come to light when tragedies occur. And so we could go on; these being only a random selection of the multitude of problems with which those in the 'front line' have to cope, in ministering to the needs of those in their care; in addition to caring for the sick, the dying and the bereaved, all of which takes time, patience, dedication, and plenty of tender loving care surrounded by prayer.

There is also the other side of the story to be considered as well, namely the everyday running of the parish with all that that implies in terms of office work for both parish and diocese which has now reached inordinate proportions, together with the increase in meetings and committees to arrange and attend. Then again, because of the fall in the number of vocations and the cost of providing clergy for parishes, the last few years have seen an increase in the grouping of parishes, often of up to five, or even six, which must be a nightmare for the priest in charge, not only in arranging and implementing service rotas, but also in attending to the needs of the church fabric; not to mention keeping an eye on the financial situation in raising the required running expenses and diocesan quotas. Nor have we touched upon the needs of the one who has to take all of these things on board, deal with them, and face the consequences; what is there in it all for him or her? We are not thinking here of any material gain or of a salary commensurate with the workload he or she has to carry; but rather of the pressures which inevitably come when so many demands are made on time effort and energy; leaving little opportunity for one's personal life and for that spiritual refreshment, growth and preparation which are so essential, and without which there can be serious consequences in frustration and mental breakdown.

All of which brings us, yet again, to the problems facing not only those whose task and responsibility it is to select and train candidates for ordination, but also to appoint those duly ordained to the 'cure of souls' in parishes; every one of which will have its own identity, personalities, peculiarities, strengths, weaknesses and challenges, and each of which needs to experience the love, mercy and forgiveness of Almighty God and to receive deeply of His Grace. It is this common need, and the ability of the particular person chosen to be the willing channel of the healing and enabling power of the Holy Spirit in meeting and fulfilling that need, which I feel must be allowed to lie at the heart, first of the selection and subsequently of the appointment procedures, rather than the seemingly inflexible pattern of selection with its emphasis on academic ability and qualifications, and the sociological and other such influential factors which are so often allowed to impinge upon, and often dominate, the system of parochial appointments. The importance of ensuring, so far as is humanly possible, that the most suitable candidate for the particular post is chosen cannot be over emphasized, and if this were to lead eventually to a complete review and overhaul of the present long standing procedures, so be it. For it would seem to me, that in a situation crying out for labourers to work in the Lord's vineyard, where the harvest is plenteous, but the labourers are few; a system which can lead to those who feel truly called by God to serve Him in the Sacred Ministry, and who have a wealth of experience in the University of Life, being rejected on the grounds of insufficient academic ability, is both flawed and in need of the review and overhaul already referred to. At the same time, it has to be acknowledged that the introduction of the Non-Stipendiary Ministry, (NSM) and the Ordained Local Ministry, (OLM) has certainly been a step in the right direction, but there is still plenty of work and thinking to be done before the review is completed to the satisfaction of all concerned.

So far in this chapter, we have thought about Discipleship, first, in terms of those who hold authority in the church as a whole with the overall responsibility for being faithful to the words and teachings of Holy Scripture in meeting the needs of our world, in what, without doubt, are desperate times, where the temptation to compromise is great and where the need to stand up and be counted on the things which really matter in life is of paramount importance. To this end, it would appear that the 'powers that be' have been weighed in the balance and have been found wanting; such that there is need for a radical change of heart, for penitence and forgiveness, for new vision, and for the courage to stand up and be counted, regardless of the cost.

Secondly, we have thought about Discipleship in terms of those who have the responsibility for the selection and training of candidates for ordination, and subsequently for their appointment in parishes; and we have expressed doubts about the present systems and the need to review and overhaul them, as necessary, to meet the pressing needs of the present day.

Thirdly, we have thought about Discipleship in terms of those at the front line, who have tremendous responsibilities laid on them, with work-loads that show an inordinate increase in administrative work over the years, that is not only time consuming, but also frustrating and debilitating; and we have seen the importance of the need to find time for one's own personal life, and for that spiritual refreshment, growth and preparation which are so essential, and without which there can be serious consequences health-wise. Bishop Morris Maddocks, in his book 'Journey to Wholeness' writes, "There was a timeless quality about the life of Jesus. His earthly life was lived in the shadow of eternity. There were thirty years of virtual silence in preparation for three years of ministry. He invariably gave himself space. A long while before day he went out alone into the hills to commune with his heavenly Father. His life was lived in contemplative stillness which allowed him to be a person of vision and realize his destiny. 'Crowds of people came to hear him and to be healed of their sicknesses. But Jesus often withdrew to lonely places and prayed' (Luke 5. verses 15-16). Not even the pressures and demands of real human need deflected him from his own spiritual journey. There is a lesson here for a church that can only see the proclamation of a social gospel as the reason for its existence." I believe the Bishop's words are both true and highly relevant to the Church and those involved in its ministry today and that his observations need to be heeded by his fellow bishops, so that they may be more aware of the needs of those at the 'sharp end' of things, that they may be given every opportunity and encouragement to put them into practice. For as Bishop Maddocks goes on to say, "The Christian leader has an obligation to put before men and women again in our time the significance of their destiny. He or she will only accomplish this if they are a person of vision, someone who has not only seen the Lord in mountain-top visions but sees him in the ordinary of life, and can so illuminate life for others that the ordinary is transfigured into the extraordinary. The destiny we are all called to fulfil is the undertaking of that journey to wholeness that leads to maturity, 'until we all reach unity in the faith and in the knowledge of the Son of God and become mature, attaining to the whole measure of the fullness of Christ' (Ephesians, chapter 4, verse 13). To attain this vision and keep it unsullied, Jesus himself had to pay the highest price, a cost that anyone must sit down and count who will follow the vision they are given. He could fulfil his destiny only at the price of loneliness, unpopularity, betrayal and eventually death on the cross, but it was for the joy that was before him that he endured; the joy that the Kingdom of heaven would be opened to all believers. His victory came through continuing on the journey. The Kingdom of God itself may well be a road, a direction, a movement, a vision. The only sure point is God, and Him reigning, revealed by Him who is 'The Way'."

We now turn to look at Discipleship from another viewpoint, namely that of those whose lot it is to be at the receiving end from those duly selected, trained, and subsequently appointed to care for them 'in the Lord'; and by way of an introduction I want to share with you a short article which appeared in the Readers Page of the Sunday Post of the 17th of October 2003, sent in by D.Eaken, Belfast; under the heading of,

Can't win!

If his sermon is a few minutes longer that usual, he sends us to sleep. If it's short, he hasn't bothered. If he raises his voice, he's shouting. If he speaks normally, you can't hear or understand a thing. If he's away, he's always on holiday. If he's always around, he never goes away. If he's out visiting, he's never at home. If he's in the house, he never visits his parishioners. If he talks finances, he's always talking about money. If he organises a bazaar, he wears everybody out. If he doesn't the parish is dead. If he takes his time with people, he goes on and on. If he's brief, he never listens. If he redecorates the church, he's wasting money. If he doesn't, he's letting things go to ruin. If he's young he lacks experience. If he's old, he ought to retire. And if he dies…well of course, nobody could ever take his place.

As we read these pearls of wisdom, we may well smile, but they are a gentle reminder that there will always be those who are never satisfied; who are always ready to criticise and to find fault, such that even the Angel Gabriel would have a rough ride. But thankfully they are few in number and in the main parishioners are willing to give the new incumbent a fair chance to show his or her mettle, and to this end, from the incumbent's point of view, it is necessary to use the first twelve months, 'the honeymoon period', wisely; in moving amongst people, getting to know them, so that the vibes are generally good for all concerned and the bush telegraph is the bearer of good news and glad tidings. Nor is it always realised that members of the congregation have only one face and one name to remember, while the new one in their midst has many faces and names to learn and to commit to memory. And because each change of staff will bring with it new thoughts and ideas for the future of the parish, it is a blessing when all concerned see the change as the opportunity for a new start. It isn't easy, but it can be a golden opportunity, not only to prevent unnecessary clashes of plans and personalities, but also for prayerful self-examination and self- assessment of the depth of our own faith and commitment; to ask ourselves where we really stand; and what we have to offer to God and His service in terms of time, talents and possessions.

In carrying out such self-examinations and self-assessments, we have to acknowledge that basically, in terms of time, talents and possessions, we are only offering back to God those things, which in truth, are His; as the Offertory prayer in Holy Communion, (Common Worship 2000) so well expresses,

Priest: Yours, Lord, is the greatness, the power,
            the glory, the splendour, and the majesty;
            for everything in heaven and on earth is yours.

All: All things come from you,
            and of your own do we give you.

Words which echo the thinking of St.Paul in his first letter to the Corinthians, chapter 4 verse 7,"For who makes you different from anyone else? What do you have that you did not receive? And if you did receive it, why do you boast as if you did not!" Our willingness to accept this truth and to make our very own free-will offering of all that we have received from God back to Him and to His service will, in itself, be a real and meaningful indication, not only of our faith and gratitude, but also of the depth of our commitment. It will involve us in looking deeply into ourselves as we are at this moment of time. It will mean asking ourselves what it is that makes us tick in the Christian and Spiritual sense; and what motives, if any, lie behind our present involvement or otherwise in the Church. It takes honesty and patience, and it also takes courage, but it needs to be done. One of the verses penned by the Scottish bard Robert Burns is very fitting here, when he writes, "O wad some Pow'r the giftie gie us to see oursels as others see us!" (Oh would some Power the gift give us to see ourselves as others see us). Again, we have all heard it said, "I don't go to church, I don't feel the need, and anyway they are mostly hypocrites who do", and perhaps unconsciously we ignore it because we don't like to think of ourselves in this way, and because in the main it is said as an excuse because those concerned don't want to be involved, they don't want to make any commitment. But what if the comment comes instead from one totally committed, a dedicated Christian in every sense of the word, whose stature as a disciple of Jesus is, without question, one of the foremost of our time. I refer yet again to David Watson with whose words we began this chapter; because again in the Introduction to his book 'Discipleship', he has something very thought provoking and challenging to say to us.

"Solzhenitsyn said on BBC Panorama in March 1976; 'I wouldn't be surprised at the sudden and imminent fall of the West....Nuclear war is not even necessary to the Soviet Union. You can be taken simply with bare hands.'

Why is that? It is because Christians in the West have largely neglected what it means to be a disciple of Christ. The vast majority of western Christians are church-members, pew fillers, hymn-singers, sermon-tasters, Bible-readers, even born-again-believers or Spirit-filled charismatics - but not true disciples of Jesus. If we were willing to learn the meaning of real discipleship and actually to become disciples, the church in the West would be transformed and the resultant impact on society would be staggering. This is no idle claim. It happened in the first century when a tiny handful of timid disciples began, in the power of the Spirit, the greatest spiritual revolution the world has ever known. Even the mighty Roman Empire yielded, within three centuries, to the power of the gospel of Christ."

I think you will agree that in the above extract, there is a great deal of food for thought for all of us. There is the challenge to take a good long hard look at our lives and not only to see, but also acknowledge, just how much his observations apply to us as individuals and collectively as the Church. All those who have been Baptised into the Body of Christ, are called and commissioned to be His disciples, but has that calling and commission been fulfilled in your life and mine? And if not, why not, and what must we be doing about it? Is it because we have not yet grasped the wonder of the personal nature of our calling? It is not something we chose to do; as Jesus said "you did not choose me, but I chose you and appointed you to go and bear fruit - fruit that will last. Then the Father will give you whatever you ask in my name. This is my command: Love each other" (St John's Gospel, chapter 15 verses 16-17).

There is therefore, something very special about our being called personally by Jesus. His call must ring as true and as real for you and for me as it did for Peter and Andrew, James and John and the rest long ago; it should not only alter our whole relationship towards our Master, but also act as a real source of motivation for the work He has given us to do. It is only when we begin to see ourselves as chosen, called and commissioned by Christ individually, that we shall have any real sense of our responsibility to give ourselves anew 'as a living sacrifice, holy and acceptable to God' (Romans, chapter 12, verse 1).

The next thing we have to remember is, that although the call of Jesus is to each of us personally, it is also a call first to Him and then into a common discipleship - a team. He calls us to share our lives both with him and with one another in love. This is why in the passage from John, chapter 15, verses 16-17 mentioned above, our Lord's statement 'you did not choose me, but I chose you' is followed almost immediately by His command to 'love each other'; and this love will have two dimensions, firstly, we are to love one another as He has loved us, and secondly, through the demonstration of our love for each other, those who see it in action will readily recognise us as the disciples of Jesus (St.John's Gospel, chapter 13, verses 34-35).

The love and the life which Jesus shares with those He calls is very special; there are no words which adequately describe the feelings of peace, joy and reassurance which are all-embracing and fulfilling and which have to be experienced to understand the wonder of them and the difficulty, nay, impossibility of trying to find words to describe them in depth, though many have tried. For example,

> JESU, the very thought of thee
> With sweetness fills my breast;
> But sweeter far thy face to see,
> And in thy presence rest.

> Nor voice can sing, nor heart can frame,
> Nor can the memory find,
> A sweeter sound than thy blest name,
> O Saviour of mankind!

O hope of every contrite heart,
O joy of all the meek,
To those who fall, how kind thou art!
How good to those who seek!

But what for those who find! Ah, this
Nor tongue nor pen can show;
The love of Jesus, what it is
None but his loved ones know.

Jesu, our only joy be thou,
As thou our prize wilt be;
Jesu, be thou our glory now,
And through eternity.

Jesu, dulcis memoria.
Latin c 12th century
Trans. Edward Caswell 1814-78

The big question we now have to ask is whether this life and love of Jesus are a living reality in our hearts and lives or not; because if they are not, then, as David Watson tried to tell us previously, in terms which, at the time, we may not have been happy with, we might very well be living under an illusion; believing that all is well and that with years of faithful Church attendance and Bible reading behind us we are perfectly equipped to be the Disciples of Jesus. But important and necessary though these things are to our spiritual growth toward maturity, they are not in themselves the answer; without the life and love of Jesus within us we are not equipped to become, or to serve, as the true Disciples of Jesus in the fullest sense of the word. And while this thought may shock us, we have nevertheless to take it seriously, and to take a good long hard look at ourselves, in the light of all that has been said, in order to see where we stand and to seek for help through meditation, prayer and sacrament; in and through which, we acknowledge our need and helplessness, and humbly ask for that divine indwelling and love which will make all the difference to us and to our work in His Name and for His sake; that life and love which transforms, redeems and forgives. We see this in action in the words of the angel to Mary Magdalene, Mary the mother of James, and Salome who were first at the empty tomb on Easter Day, "go, tell his disciples and Peter, 'He is going ahead of you into Galilee. There you will see him, just as he told you.'" (St.Mark's Gospel chapter 16, verse 7), and we note the special word of encouragement to Simon Peter, who must still have been feeling wretched following his threefold denial of his Lord and Master in the early hours of Good Friday morning. Then again, in the various resurrection appearances, Jesus came to the disciples, individually and as a group; to Mary Magdalene at the tomb, (St John's Gospel chapter 20, verses 10-18) to the disciples, in the Upper Room, (St John's Gospel chapter 20, verses 19-29) and by the lakeside, (St John's Gospel. Chapter 21,verses 1-14) and to the two disciples on the road to Emmaus, (St Luke's Gospel chapter 24, verses 13-35); in every instance to assure them of His living presence, and of His love and forgiveness, gifts so vital and precious to His disciples both then and now.

The call by Jesus to discipleship has other dimensions as well. From the moment they accept Him as Lord and Saviour, He expects from every disciple of His, unconditional obedience for the rest of their lives. As He makes very clear in St Matthew's Gospel chapter 7 verse 21, "Not everyone who says to me, 'Lord, Lord,' will enter the kingdom of heaven, but only he who does the will of my Father who is in heaven.", and also in St. Luke's Gospel chapter 6 verse 46, "Why do you call me, 'Lord, Lord,' and do not do what I say?" These are not the words of a despot calling for unconditional surrender or else, but rather of the One who realises that to obey God's will is to find true, real and lasting fulfilment in our lives. If the Church is to stand any real chance at all of meeting, and dealing with, the enormous problems and temptations of the twenty-first century, in and through the power of the Holy Spirit, there is an urgent need for true disciples who will bind themselves to Jesus Christ in unswerving obedience and loyalty.

The call by Jesus to discipleship is also a call to serve. We see this in the call of those first disciples of His and His commission to them. In the tenth chapter of St. Matthew's Gospel we read, Verse 1, "He called his twelve disciples to him and gave them authority to drive out evil spirits and to heal every disease and sickness," and in verses 7-8, "As you go, preach this message: 'The kingdom of heaven is near.' Heal the sick, raise the dead, cleanse those who have leprosy, drive out demons. Freely you have received, freely give." But the list is not yet complete and for it to be so we have to turn to St Matthew's Gospel, chapter 28 verse 16 to the end, in what has become known as the Great Commission, "Then the eleven disciples - by this time Judas was dead and had not been replaced - went to Galilee, to the mountain where Jesus had told them to go. When they saw him, they worshipped him; but some doubted. Then Jesus came to them and said, 'All authority in heaven and on earth has been given to me. Therefore go and make disciples of all nations, baptising them in the name of the Father and of the Son and of the Holy Spirit, and teaching them to obey everything I have commanded you. And surely I am with you always, to the very end of the age.'"

When we think of the call to serve as it applied to the first disciples of Jesus, there were occasions when He had to correct them because they had got hold of the wrong end of the stick! In St Mark's Gospel, chapter 9 verses 33 - 35 we read, "They came to Capernaum. When he was in the house, he asked them, 'What were you arguing about on the road?' But they kept quiet because on the way they had argued about who was the greatest. Sitting down, Jesus called the Twelve and said, 'If anyone wants to be first, he must be the very last, and the servant of all.'" There was also the quest for status among them in the persons of James and John, the Sons of Zebedee, who, together with Simon Peter and Andrew, were members of what we might call the inner circle, and who for one reason or another sought for further advancement. In St Mark's Gospel, the first to be written and very much influenced by St.Peter, it is the two brothers themselves who approach Jesus, (chapter 10 verses 35-40) whereas in St Mathew's account of the same incident, it is Salome their mother who approaches Him on their behalf (chapter 20 verses 20-23); the reason for the difference probably lying in the fact that Matthew was anxious not to offend two of his fellow disciples, while Mark on the other hand, like Peter has no such qualms and tells it as it really happened. Whatever the reason for the difference, the object of the exercise was the same, namely that James and John be allowed to sit, one at each side of Jesus in His kingdom, and in that Mark's account is the earliest, we will follow it through with him. "You do not know what you are asking," Jesus said, "Can you drink the cup I drink or be baptised with the baptism I am baptised with?" "We can," they answered. Jesus said to them, "You will drink the cup I drink and be baptised with the baptism I am baptised with, but to sit at my right or left is not for me to grant. These places belong to those for whom they have been prepared by my Father." What Jesus is endeavouring to show James and John is that their quest is misguided, that their ambition in this respect is in the spirit of the world; they are looking for status instead of service. When the rest of the disciples heard this, they became indignant with the two brothers, and so Jesus called them together and said, "You know that those who are regarded as rulers of the Gentiles lord it over them, and their high officials exercise authority over them. Not so with you. Instead, whoever wants to become great among you must be your servant, and whoever wants to be first must be slave of all. For even the Son of Man (Jesus Himself) did not come to be served, but to serve, and to give his life as a ransom for many" (verses 42-45). Later they were to see His words demonstrated, in a never-to-be-forgotten way, when at the Last Supper He wrapped a towel round His waist and washed their feet.

The element of ambition, however, was not the only one among the disciples; we also find the element of self-pity. Even the 'Big Fisherman', Simon Peter, when he began to realise and feel the considerable cost of discipleship, supplies us with a good example of this when he says to Jesus, "We have left all we had to follow you!" And in reply he is given reassurance by Jesus that those who do the same as they have done will be duly compensated. "no-one who has left home or wife or brothers or parents or children for the sake of the kingdom of God will fail to receive many times as much in this age and, in the age to come, eternal life" (St Luke's Gospel, chapter 18 verses 28-30). One is also reminded here to a lesser extent of St Paul and what he referred to as his "thorn in the flesh", about the cause of which there have been several speculations, but whatever it was it certainly brought him to his knees from time to time. In 2 Corinthians chapter 12 verses 7-9, he calls it " a messenger of Satan to torment me," "Three times I pleaded with the Lord to take it away from me." But he said to me, "My grace is sufficient for you, for my power is made perfect in weakness." No doubt there are many more examples than these from the pages of Holy Scripture, and no doubt we could add to their number from our own experiences, not least in those times when we have felt inadequate or unworthy; suffice it here to have made reference to self-pity as a real feature to be identified and dealt with. Nor can we leave this particular element without spending a moment or two in thinking how those first disciples felt at being sent out to face the world. They must have felt it a daunting proposition to say the least, and at times they must have felt overwhelmed by it all.

At the beginning of chapter one of his fascinating book, 'Ambassador for Christ', Dr.William Barclay writes, "After Jesus had done his work on earth and had returned to his Father, the total number of his followers amounted to 120 people (Acts Chapter 1, verse 15). To that 120 people was entrusted a task that was enough to daunt the bravest heart, for they were told to go out and win every man in the world for Christ. To take nothing but Jews, there were in Palestine at the time about 4,000,000. That is to say of Jews alone fewer than 1 in 30,000 were Christians. Palestine was a little country, not more than 40 miles from west to east and not more than 120 miles from north to south. Out of that little country this insignificant band of ordinary folk had the duty laid on them of winning the untold millions of the world for Christ." Dr.Barclay then goes on to tell us how, "In the year A.D.64 there fell upon the Christians the first of the great persecutions under Emperor Nero. Tacitus, the Roman historian, tells us that in that persecution 'a vast multitude of Christians' fell to the fury of persecution." But this did not deter the rest in their work, and one can only wonder at the phenomenal success those first disciples achieved, and from it the Church today needs to learn and to take heart, called as it is, and called as we are to discipleship in our own day and age! The needs of the world are vast. God in His love longs to reach out to all those who, inwardly or outwardly, are crying out for help; but He has chosen to work primarily through the disciples of Jesus. If they are taken up with their own personal needs as first priority, or if they are looking for position and status in the church rather than a life of self-giving, they will be of no use to God. They are called to serve; and a servant must be prepared to go where his master sends him and do what his master commands.

When we look at life today, with the many problems, frustrations, and pressures that come from living in our modern high-speed world, it stands out in sharp contrast to the relative simplicity of the life of Jesus. He laid aside all earthly security and material comforts; there were even times when He had nowhere to lay His head down to sleep as we read in St Matthew chapter 8 verse 20 and St Luke chapter 9 verse 58, "Foxes have holes and birds of the air have nests, but the Son of Man has nowhere to lay his head." Jesus lived in total dependence on His Father's love and faithfulness, and He also called His disciples to do the same, He called them to a simple way of life, a life of humility and poverty, and He told them that although it was the Father's good pleasure to give them the kingdom (St Luke's Gospel chapter 12 verse 32), they were to sell their possessions and give to the poor and in so doing provide for themselves purses that would not wear out, a treasure in heaven that would not be exhausted, where no thief could come near and no moth destroy. For where their treasure was, so would their heart be also (verses 33-34). Like their Lord and Master they had to be willing to leave their homes, their families, their occupations, their securities - everything for the sake of the Kingdom of God. But if they were willing to do this and if they made the Kingdom of God their top priority, all they needed would be provided for them. In all this they had to trust their Heavenly Father and be anxious for nothing. Having said this, we must remind ourselves that what has been said in this paragraph refers primarily to the first disciples of Jesus who were living with Him; but in essence it also applies to His disciples of every age. The call is to live as simple a life as possible, with complete trust in God, that He in turn will supply all our needs - not wants - and consequently we are not to be anxious about anything. In St.Luke's second work, the Book of the Acts of the Apostles we have at least two good examples of how the early church responded to this call. In Chapter 2 verses 42-47, we read, "They devoted themselves to the apostles' teaching and fellowship, to the breaking of bread and to prayer. Everyone was filled with awe, and many wonders and miraculous signs were done by the apostles. All the believers were together and had everything in common. Selling their possessions and goods, they gave to anyone as he had need. Every day they continued to meet together in the temple courts. They broke bread in their homes and ate together with glad and sincere hearts, praising God and enjoying the favour of all the people. And the Lord added to their number daily those who were being saved." Then, in chapter 4 verses 32 - 37 we read, "All the believers were one in heart and mind. No-one claimed that any of his possessions was his own, but they shared everything they had. With great power the apostles continued to testify to the resurrection of the Lord Jesus, and much grace was upon them all. There were no needy persons among them. For from time to time, those who owned lands or houses sold them, brought the money from the sales and put it at the feet of the apostles and it was distributed to anyone as he had need. Joseph, a Levite from Cyprus, whom the apostles called Barnabas (which means Son of Encouragement), sold a field he owned and brought the money and put it at the apostles' feet." And just by way of warning to those tempted to hold something back from the proceeds for themselves, chapter 5 verses 1-10, tells the story of the fate of Ananias and his wife Sapphira, who were tempted to do just that; as if to say, 'let the reader beware.'

If we compare the above readings with our present day situation, it is easy to see how the affluence of many Christians today, especially in the West, is a potential stumbling-block to effective and radical discipleship; just as the comparative wealth of the western churches is not only a stumbling-block to their unity but also to their Christian outreach and witness to the rest of the world. It is only as we seek first the Kingdom of God and His righteousness, that through the guidance of the Holy Spirit we will be enabled to understand His will for us and for the world, and to learn how to share with those in need, all that God in His bountiful goodness has given to us, for He loves a cheerful giver. (2 Corinthians chapter 9 verse 7) And furthermore, it is unlikely that God will entrust us with the true riches of His spiritual life and power until we have proved our stewardship of material things; until our priorities are based on our genuinely serving Him, the author and giver of all good gifts, and not the gifts themselves. It is then that He will entrust us with the gifts of His Holy Spirit, which will enrich beyond measure our own lives as well as those of the ones we are called to serve.

No thoughts about the call by Jesus to discipleship would be complete, without reference to the aspect of sacrifice and suffering. In the sixteenth chapter of the Gospel of St.Matthew, verses 13-20 we read about St.Peter's confession of Jesus as "the Christ, the Son of the living God." Then in verse 21 Jesus predicts His death, and in verse 22 He is rebuked by Peter "never Lord!" he said "this shall never happen to you," and in turn in verse 23 Peter is then rebuked by Jesus, "Get behind me Satan! You are a stumbling block to me; you do not have in mind the things of God, but the things of men." We may wonder how we would have reacted in Peter's shoes, and possibly moreso when Jesus goes on to say in verses 24 - 25, "If anyone would come after me, he must deny himself and take up his cross and follow me. For whoever wants to save his life will lose it, but whoever loses his life for me will find it." There is no hesitancy here, no making apologies, these are the stark facts; the call of Jesus involves the willingness to follow Him to suffering and even to death. As St Paul underlines in Chapter 1 verse 29 of his letter to the Philippians, " For it has been granted to you on behalf of Christ not only to believe on him, but also to suffer for him." Nor is St Paul afraid to point out what all of this meant for him in practical terms. In his second letter to the Corinthians chapter 11 verses 23 - 31, he catalogues his experiences, "I have worked much harder, been in prison more frequently, been flogged more severely, and been exposed to death again and again. Five times I received from the Jews the forty lashes minus one. Three times I was beaten with rods, once I was stoned, three times I was shipwrecked, I spent a night and a day in the open sea, I have been constantly on the move. I have been in danger from rivers, in danger from bandits, in danger from my own countrymen, in danger from Gentiles; in danger in the city, in danger in the country, in danger at sea; and in danger from false brothers. I have laboured and toiled and have often gone without sleep; I have known hunger and thirst and have often gone without food; I have been cold and naked. Besides everything else I face daily the pressure of my concern for all the churches. Who is weak, and I do not feel weak? Who is led into sin, and I do not inwardly burn? If I must boast, I will boast of the things that show my weakness. The God and Father of the Lord Jesus, who is to be praised forever knows that I am not lying." Is it any wonder then, that in verse 17 of chapter 6 of his letter to the Galatians, he can say, "From henceforth let no man trouble me; for I bear in my body the marks of the Lord Jesus"(King James Version). Neither is St Paul alone: according to various Christian traditions and writings too numerous to detail, most if not all of the apostles suffered privations and eventual martyrdom of one form or another, and up until around A.D.305, the early church suffered waves of bitter and at times appalling persecution from a succession of Roman emperors. But suffering for disciples of Jesus, is not limited to that period, but has been a constant thread running through history to the present day, where quite regularly we hear of atrocities of one kind or another. In recent years thousands of Christians have been imprisoned and tortured for their faith, and it has been estimated by several sources that there were more martyrdoms for Christ in the 20th Century than in the rest of the church's history! Suffering then, is inextricably bound up with, and woven through discipleship in a way which in time will embrace us all, if it hasn't already done so, and yet we will not be the first to discover that so very often it is in the midst of suffering that God shows Himself to us in a deeper and more real way than perhaps we have experienced before. We must rest in the Lord and wait patiently for Him, knowing that in all our sufferings for Him, He will never fail us or forsake us, and that with our hand in His we have nothing to fear, as St Paul reassures us in his letter to the Romans chapter 8 verses 38-39, "For I am convinced that neither death nor life, nor angels, nor demons, neither the present nor the future, nor any powers, neither height nor depth, nor anything else in all creation, will be able to separate us from the love of God that is in Christ Jesus our Lord."

So we see that in thinking about the various facets of discipleship we have a great deal of food for thought and, in addition, we would do well to read what Jesus has to say about the cost of being a disciple in St Luke's Gospel chapter 14 verses 25-34, as part of our onward thinking and study.

We began this chapter by asking how the Church as a whole is dealing with the demands of the 21st Century A.D, and perhaps we may have felt tempted to vent our feelings in this respect; perhaps now, in view of our thoughts on Discipleship, we ought to be asking ourselves the same question. What progress have we made in our own spiritual pilgrimage, if any, and what visible effect have we personally had, if any, in furthering the work of those first disciples of Jesus? Do we have the strength and courage to face the overwhelming odds as they did, and to step out in faith and in the power of the Holy Spirit, to live and work to God's praise and glory? As we think on these things, as I hope and pray we will, let it be prayerfully in those beautiful words of St.Ignatius Loyola,

Teach us, good Lord, to serve you as you deserve,
to give and not to count the cost;
to fight and not to heed the wounds;
to toil and not to seek for rest;
to labour and not to ask for any reward,
save that of knowing that we do your will,
through Jesus Christ our Lord

Amen.

CHAPTER FIVE

In St.Matthew's Gospel, chapter 25, verses 31-33, Jesus introduces His parable of the Sheep and the Goats by saying, "When the Son of Man (Jesus Himself) comes in his glory, and all the angels with him, he will sit on his throne in heavenly glory. All the nations will be gathered before him, and he will separate the people one from another as a shepherd separates the sheep from the goats. He will put the sheep on his right and the goats on his left." He then continues in verses 34-40 by saying -

"Then the King will say to those on his right hand,
'Come, you who are blessed by my Father; take your
inheritance, the kingdom prepared for you since the creation
of the world. For I was hungry and you gave me something
to eat, I was thirsty and you gave me something to drink, I was
a stranger and you invited me in, I needed clothes and you
clothed me, I was sick and you looked after me, I was in prison
and you came to visit me.'
Then the righteous will answer him, 'Lord, when did we
see you hungry and feed you, or thirsty and give you something
to drink? When did we see you a stranger and invite you in, or
needing clothes and clothe you? When did we see you sick or
in prison and go to visit you?'
The king will reply, 'I tell you the truth, whatever you did
for one of the least of these brothers of mine, you did for me.'"

Having dealt with those on His right hand, the Sheep, the righteous, Jesus then goes on to deal in verses 41-45 with those on His left hand, the Goats, the unrighteous, who, because they have, by the sin of omission, failed to help others in time of need, have, by the same token, failed to help Him; and as a result are, in the words of verse 41, left in no doubt as to their fate. "Depart from me, you who are cursed, into the eternal fire prepared for the devil and his angels." Very harsh words indeed from the King of Love, and yet words which underline how seriously Jesus took the second and great commandment to love one's neighbour as oneself, to mean more than mere words, but rather to be seen as faith in action. There is also the added bonus for those who are faithful in this respect, in that they will experience, in a very real way, that whatever they do for others in His Name, they are in fact doing personally for Him, and with it the inner joy, peace and fulfilment this can and does bring to their hearts and lives. This needs to be the canon, the measuring rod, if you like, which we must use in assessing our own success or lack of it with respect to our neighbourliness toward others; and each of us will have to look back at our own experiences, not only to make that assessment, but also to make reassessments and readjustments to ensure that as far as possible we can do better in the future.

When I was asked during my selection conference, "why are you here?" because, in the opinion of the questioner, "academically, I had nothing to offer", I gave two reasons, namely "because I love God and because I love His children"; and whilst these have been at the forefront of my mind and the underlying thrust to all that I have said and endeavoured to do ever since, there have certainly been times when they have been sorely tested not only in the various ministries in which I have been privileged to serve, in parishes, in hospitals, in prisons and in a hospice here in England, together with experiences in South India and to a much lesser extent in Cyprus; but also in the eight years or so when I suffered from severe, often manic depression; a period in my life which not only had a profound effect on me and my family, but also because of the positive lessons it taught me for the future. It began to rear its ugly head towards the end of my period as Curate of Standish. It was then the practice in the diocese to serve two curacies, but because of my family situation and the fact that my mother-in-law was now living with us, we needed a bigger house than those usually provided and, because St. Wilfrid's House fitted the bill admirably, I was allowed to stay for the full curacy term of 5 years. I would also like to think that my work there to date made the decision much easier for those who had the responsibility for making it! For several years before my arrival in Standish, it had become the trend to have two curates in training, so that together with the Rector it was very much a team ministry situation in which I 'blossomed', if that is the right term to use, so that when thoughts were turned to the desirability of my having a church of my own, I began to feel threatened and pressurised. I so loved the people and work in Standish, that had it been suggested that I stayed as Perpetual Curate, I would gladly have accepted in that I did not share the view that it was necessary to move on to bigger and better things. But it was not to be and I had no choice, except in so far that I was to visit one or two parishes either vacant or soon to be so, in order to see if any of them appealed to me. When I first visited the Parish of St. Paul, Low Moor, one of the three Church of England parishes in Clitheroe, the church itself felt warm and welcoming, even though it was empty, and I felt very much drawn to it, it felt right and I returned home feeling that if I had to move, this was as good a place as any to work and make our home. When subsequently I met with the then Parochial Church Council and had discussions with the members of it, I began to realise the vast amount of love, prayer, and effort the task before me was going to involve and it would have been easy to go on to look for other things, but I decided to accept the challenge and agreed to go there.

There is a saying that 'hard work never killed anyone', but it certainly took its toll in my case, as no doubt it also has in countless other cases as well, and after many visits to the G.P, I was referred to Dr.E.T.Downham, Consultant Psychologist at Burnley General Hospital, whose opening words I will never forget; "how do you come to be troubled with depression? You have the easiest job in the world, my father was a parson and I know!" I remember wondering what kind of a parson his father had been and whether the parish life he was accustomed to bore any resemblance to mine; furthermore, the flippancy of his opening comment certainly did not fill me with confidence for my future in his hands! I was subsequently proved right, in that efforts to ascertain the trigger for my illness, together with drug therapy, mainly with anti-depressants and examination under the truth drug, proved fruitless, and two and a half courses (fourteen treatments) of Electro-Convulsive Therapy, commonly referred to as 'shock treatment', failed to provide any relief whatsoever, and I was sent home to face a very uncertain future both for myself and for the family too. It was a dark and dismal time for all of us. I did receive a visit from the Rev. Leonard Cragg, later Canon Cragg, who had been the Chaplain of the then Whittingham Hospital for the mentally ill, and who later became Vicar of Lytham Parish Church. I had known Len for some years and it was good of him to take the time to visit and to try to help as much as he could. Looking back to this time, I recall how he chain-smoked throughout the whole visit and I remember wondering which of us really needed help the most! The Vicar of one of our neighbouring parishes, that of St.James, the Rev.Kenneth Broadhurst, together with his wife Shirley, also did their best to help, and it was through them that I went to see the well-known Clinical Psychologist Professor Frank Lake at Nottingham University. One of Professor Lake's theories was that many cases of depression such as mine were the result of difficulties and pressures experienced during the birth process, and that because of my being born with a Cleft Palate and Hare Lip, there was a distinct probability that I was a good candidate for this category. Following the consultation, he proceeded, with the help of colleagues in a darkened room, to take me stage by stage through the birth process from beginning to end. It was a frightening and exhausting experience. Once again I was a baby experiencing pain and stress in struggling to be free of the confines of the birth canal that held me so tightly, and then the tremendous relief of entry into the world! It left me feeling like a wrung out mop and although it involved a great deal of effort on the part of all concerned, sadly it did not help in providing a solution to the problem I had; but it did help me to appreciate something of what is meant when we hear of babies being in distress during the birth process resulting in surgical intervention to alleviate it. The experience also gave me a new insight into the story of Jesus and Nicodemus, a ruler of the Jews and a secret disciple of Jesus (St.John chapter 3 verses1-15). Nicodemus came to Jesus by night and said "Rabbi, we know that you are a teacher who has come from God. For no-one could perform the miraculous signs you are doing, if God were not with him." In reply Jesus declared, " I tell you the truth, no-one can see the kingdom of God unless he is born again." "How can a man be born when he is old?" Nicodemus asked. "Surely he cannot enter a second time into his mother's womb to be born." From the purely physical point of view Nicodemus would appear to have a valid argument, but had he had the benefit of a visit to Professor Frank Lake, he may just have seen things in a different light!

Only those who have suffered the rigours and debilitating effects of depression in its fullest sense, as distinct from feeling depressed or 'down', can really understand what it is all about. The feelings of loneliness, desolation and hopelessness that can so quickly, and often without warning, plunge one into deep despair, often with overwhelming feelings of guilt, unworthiness and worthlessness, are those of which every depressive will have had some experience; whilst for the manic depressive, there is also the mood swing from despair to euphoria, when without explanation or fore-thought one feels compelled to attempt things which the depressed state could never even contemplate, and which in turn, when they backfire, return one into the mire in a more deeper way than before! In between times, there are the disturbed nights, continually in and out of bed, pacing the bedroom floor, striving to get out of the tunnel of darkness with no glimpse of light at the end of it,

not to mention awakening in the morning to those negative thoughts which
rapidly follow on, one from the other, in what I came to speak of as the
steamroller effect, from their ready ability to crush and to roll over one in their
unrelenting pressure, to which one feels powerless to respond. Even though
for the depressive there is the temptation to hide away under the bedclothes
feigning sleep and secretly hoping that it will eventually come to overwhelm
the mental anguish and to bring peace, if only for a little while, the steamroller
effect often does have a positive effect in making one get up to face the real
world, instead of the world in which for the rest of the time he or she is a
virtual prisoner, the world which raises problem after problem and offers no
solutions. For me it was also a twilight world in the sense that in spite of
all that was happening I was able to carry out the basic requirements of my
ministerial and priestly duties, and even though at times it was extremely
difficult and I arrived for services at the very last minute, nevertheless there
were no disasters in so far as I was aware, and to the casual observer things
appeared to be progressing favourably - more by the grace of God than by
good management I can assure you! As mentioned towards the end of chapter
one I had further complications following the death of my mother, when an
attack of shingles in my throat travelled up the ear canal killing the seventh
nerve on the right side of my face and leaving me with a facial paralysis which
eventually required corrective plastic surgery; the success of which was only
partial, but a great improvement on what had happened and helped to restore
self confidence, even though I still cannot move my right eyebrow and have
a one-sided smile! As also mentioned earlier the illness resulted in my leaving
Low Moor to return to Walton-le dale and to secular employment with the
Bishop's permission to officiate as and when I felt able to do so.

The depressions were to continue for a further three years, and pressures
continued to mount, particularly for my wife who, to date, together with
the family had suffered more than enough from the pressures of living with
a depressive; the opposite side of the coin to the one I was experiencing, but
just as painful and debilitating with all the added frustrations of feeling so
helpless. In addition to this, Audrey also had to bear the brunt of her mother,
a loving, much loved and prayerful lady, falling ill, and our eldest daughter
Janet becoming a victim to Anorexia just six months after her marriage
to Mick; an illness which was to last for six years and which at one stage
was critical with her weighing just over four stones. Janet at times was very
confused with no confidence and very much like a child who needed to be led

every step of the way, even in the simplest of things, and such was her state of mind that at one stage she also suffered an accidental overdose. How Audrey managed to cope during this period in our married life only God knows, but the day came when it was all too much for her. I had been admitted into the Psychiatric Ward at Sharoe Green Hospital in Preston and was home on leave. What was said or what happened I cannot recall in detail, suffice it to say that she simply said, "that's it, I've had enough" and walked out! I felt shocked and helpless and sat there wondering what this all meant and what I was going to do about it. One thing was certain I could not manage or go on without her; I dashed out of the house but she was nowhere to be seen. After a frantic search I eventually found her and pleaded with her to return, which thank God she did, and we sat and talked and shared a kiss and a hug as our hope and pledge for a new beginning, little knowing that there were other forces at work!

Throughout my ministry as a Licensed Reader, Deacon and Priest, I have always seen prayer, and in particular prayers for the sick, as a vital part of that ministry, bearing in mind our Lord's command to His disciples that the healing of the sick is to take its rightful place alongside the preaching of the Gospel! For example in St. Matthew's Gospel, chapter 10 verses 7-8, we read, "As you go, preach this message: 'The kingdom of heaven is near.' Heal the sick, raise the dead, cleanse those who have leprosy, drive out demons. Freely you have received, freely give." Again in St.Luke's Gospel, chapter 9 verse 2, Jesus sends out the Twelve "to preach the kingdom of God and to heal the sick," and in chapter 10, verses 8-9 we read, "When you enter a town and are welcomed, eat what is set before you. Heal the sick who are there and tell them, 'the kingdom of God is near you.'" Such that it would appear clear that for Jesus, preaching and healing are to be considered of equal importance, 'preach and heal.' A thought taken up underlined and expounded by the Reverend Canon Roy Lawrence in his fascinating book 'Christian Healing Rediscovered', in which he is not afraid to face the many problems posed by the various concepts of healing, and to express his belief that "if Jesus has given his Church two equally important commands. 'preach and heal', then the Church has become lopsided. We preach our heads off - after a fashion - but the study and practice of healing has largely been lost over the centuries." It is a fascinating read, and I recommend it to you without any hesitation whatsoever.

My own sense of the importance of prayer and particularly of praying for and with the sick, led me gently into the Ministry of Healing through prayer and the laying on of hands, after the manner of Jesus and of the Apostles in the early church; and here I cite two examples of what happened through me as the willing channel of God's love and healing power.

The first is from my time as Curate of Standish. We had only just returned from holiday and were about to start unpacking, when there was a knock on the front door. I opened it to find a very worried looking Miss Maybury, Head Mistress of the Infant's school which stood next door to St. Wilfrid's House, and where our younger daughter Linda was a scholar. In her class was a little boy by the name of John Fairhurst, with whom she was the best of friends, and the reason for Miss Maybury's visit was to tell me that John was seriously ill in the children's ward in Whelley Hospital in Wigan, and that the Doctor in charge of him had told his parents that there was nothing more that they could do for him! I had visited the hospital previously on many occasions and usually drove into the grounds to the particular ward or wards I had to visit, but on this occasion, for no particular reason, I parked on the roadway outside and made my way on foot to Barnish Ward. It was not far, but in the short time it took, two things happened. The first was that without doubt I heard a voice saying to me, "they may have given him up, but I haven't" and secondly I knew that I had to lay hands on John and pray for his healing. When I saw him for the first time I did not recognise him. I was told that he was suffering from Steven-Johnson Syndrome, the spelling of which I am unsure, which apparently only attacks little boys, or so I understood. While in India I had experienced the ravages of Leprosy but nothing like this, for there in front of me was a large scab of a body with only small and unaffected areas, and the thought of having to lay hands on him filled me with shock. But I knew that was what I had to do, for John's need far outweighed my own natural hesitancy and inner squirming, and in any case how would I ever be able to justify to myself not obeying the unmistakeable instruction I had been given? But that was never an issue, and as I ministered to John in the only way I knew how, I felt a deep peace and reassurance surrounding us both, a peace and reassurance which stayed with me as I journeyed home, and there shared all that had happened with Audrey. Later, when John's parents visited him, they were told that I had spent time with him, but no details because no member of staff was there at the time, and that an hour after I had left there had been a marked change in his condition for the better, which now gave hope for them and for all who were caring for him. From then on the improvement continued and eventually John returned home and back to school to be with

Linda and his other friends. He is now grown up and possibly married with a family of his own, I don't know, but I do know that the only sign he carries of his ordeal is that he has no eyelashes due to the high doses of drugs he had been given during his treatment. I shared with his parents all that had happened and together we gave thanks to God for His love and healing power for John, and for the precious privilege I had of being the willing channel for it

The second incident I want to relate to you happened during my time as Vicar of Low Moor. Inside the front cover of the Parish Magazine was a short note to indicate that in time of need, I could be contacted at any time of day or night, and surprisingly enough, during my five years in the Parish this was used, but never abused. In the early hours of the particular morning with which we are concerned, it was a call from Mrs.Phyllis Metcalfe, who lived in the neighbouring parish of St.James, and with whom at that moment of time I had only a passing acquaintance from her occasional attendance at church functions in our parish. She was deeply troubled as she told me that her husband Reg, a stalwart at St.James' had been admitted to Queen's Park Hospital in Blackburn, suffering from a severe Cerebral Haemorrhage from which, following a sudden relapse, he was now not expected to survive the night. She had just received an urgent call from the hospital and had ordered a taxi to take her and she was ringing to ask if I would go with her to pray for him; without any hesitation I agreed to do so and to leave any possible repercussions regarding trespassing over parish boundaries to a later date! When we arrived Reg was deeply unconscious and we soon realised that the call from the hospital had come none too early; indeed all the way there I had been hoping and praying that we would be in time, and that this was not a case, as so often happens, and indeed did happen in the case of my own brother, of the family being called after the patient has already died, on the pretext that to tell them the truth would be a great shock and could result in an accident on the way there. Fortunately this was not the case, but it did mean that the need for prayer for healing with the laying on of hands was imminent and together, gently and lovingly, we did just that for Reg and for the Lord he loved so much. We then stayed with him for quite a while, before giving him a Blessing and leaving him to rest in the Lord. We arrived back at their house at daybreak, only to discover that Phyllis had misplaced her keys! This resulted in my having to borrow a ladder and a knife from a neighbour who very fortunately was an early riser on that particular morning, and to make entry through the rear bedroom window. Even with all the strain and concern, it brought a smile when we thought of the headlines that could appear in the local Clitheroe Advertiser as a consequence, but we were spared our blushes! The next twenty-four hours were crucial, and when these passed without further complications the worst was over, Reg regained consciousness and was soon on the road to a full recovery, none the worse for the experience, and full of thanksgiving to Almighty God for the Healing touch of the Lord Jesus upon him. Once again I felt so privileged to have been a real part of the healing process and a willing channel for it. But the story did not end there! Phyllis and Reg were so moved by all that had happened, that they wanted their thanksgiving to be both prayerful and practical; they sold their home and moved into our parish, where they were regular worshippers and in time Reg was appointed as one of the Churchwardens and contributed a great deal to the life and outreach of the church and parish, with Phyllis playing her part as well. Both of them were saddened by my illness and did their very best to support us as a family both practically and prayerfully, and when the time came for us to leave they kept in touch. But the story did not end there either, in that Phyllis and particularly Reg had been so moved by all that had happened to him, that they too had developed a very healthy interest in the Ministry of Healing and as such had read any books they could find on the subject, - I was going to say any books they could lay their hands on, but I felt this might confuse the issue! And eventually this led to another incident I want to relate for you.

You will recall how, earlier in this chapter, we left off thinking about the personal and family aspects of the effects of depression at the point where I had found Audrey who had walked out of the house when the pressures on her had become so great that she felt that she could not take any more, and that we had sat down to talk and had pledged ourselves to a new beginning, ending with the words "little knowing that there were other forces at work!" Well, within days I began to feel better, the depression, which had been the cause of so much darkness and suffering in all of our lives, was lifted and gone, never to return, and I was home and free - Praise the Lord!

Four weeks later, there was a telephone call from Reg, asking if he and Phyllis could come over and see us; he was thrilled to learn that I was well again and I assured him that they were most welcome and that we would be glad to see them; but when they arrived, they were not their usual selves, and so it didn't take long for me to ask if there was something wrong. No, there is nothing wrong, but we are afraid that we have been rather deceitful, and have done something behind your back, and we cannot rest until we have told you about it and cleared the slate!

They then went on to relate how St.James' Church in Clitheroe had invited the Rev. Roy Lawrence to conduct a healing mission there, and because Phyllis and Reg had borrowed and read all the books I had on the subject, including 'Christian Healing Rediscovered' by the man himself, they were keen to attend even though they had not attended anything like it before. They naturally felt rather apprehensive, but undaunted by it all, they went to the mission, and when eventually the invitation had come to those feeling the need to receive healing through the laying on of hands with prayer, they had both responded and gone forward, not for themselves, but by proxy, for me! And now, here they both were, this very special lovely couple, apologising to me for what they saw as being deceitful! I say apologising to me, because Audrey already knew that they had done this; it all happened at the time of the crisis for us I have told you about, and they had rung her a day or so afterwards to tell her; she had known nothing previously, and it was agreed that nothing should be said to me then, so as not to give me any further pressure! "How can you feel as you do," I asked them, "when you have done something so wonderful for me and for us as a family", and together we thanked and praised the Lord. I could tell, as I saw the look on their faces, that they were now experiencing something of what I had felt when I was the willing channel for His wonderful, loving, healing power; and because they are both with Him now in the kindlier world, I pray that they will accept this sharing of all that happened with you, as a real and lasting token of our love and gratitude to them both.

One cannot experience the things I have mentioned above - and there are many others, some of which may emerge later - without acknowledging their impact on us and on our family, and without endeavouring to see how they fit into the overall scheme of things; not in the sense of asking why such things happen to us, because I know the negativity of such an approach and that for so many before me the search has been fruitless and frustrating; but rather for what purpose do they happen, and what have they to teach us, which in turn can be used to help others in the same predicament? In retrospect, although at the time 'the night was dark' and in so many ways we felt 'far from home', nevertheless we can now echo for ourselves the words of the Psalmist when he wrote, " Blessed is the man whose strength is in thee: in whose heart are thy ways. Who going through the vale of misery use it for a well: and the pools are filled with water." (Psalm 84.verses 5-6 in the Book of Common Prayer as proposed in 1928) In other words although it was an horrendous experience at the time, like in so many ways having to pass through the 'refiner's fire', the end product has been that deeper grasp on life and the ability to empathise with others in their trouble and dilemma, in a more simple, realistic and sensitive way than would have been possible before, and which has become a cause for thanksgiving, rather than a cause for regret that it ever happened to us. If I were to try to give you an illustration to help you to understand it would be this. When life is good and carefree, the tendency is to look around and to enjoy to the full the natural and material things that surround you, very often without any sense of need to say thank you to God for His Blessings in so many ways and forms. In the full energy and vitality of life we can climb the highest mountain and enjoy the view that on a good day can appear endless, but only to the limit of our own sight! It is when we go out into the darkness on a clear night and look up into the heavens for light, that our whole vision so often impaired by earthly and material things, is able to see not tens or hundreds of miles, but millions of miles! Such a thought, I believe, also applies at the heart of depression in that so often our Heavenly Father, can and does use the darkness in life to show His love and purpose for us in a more real and meaningful way than we so often prevent Him from doing in the light; when we feel we can see for ourselves where our lives are going and so do not look up to Him, as we should, for His guidance, healing and protection. This was a great help to us both in my time of illness, and it has also been a great source of strength to our younger daughter Linda in her battle with manic depression over the past few years; a very dark period for her, into which the healing power of God has now shone to bring her back to health and to give her at forty years of age the added blessing of motherhood, for which she has always longed, in the birth of Alfie Alan six weeks early on 21st May 2004, the thirty-seventh anniversary of my admission as Deacon into the Sacred Ministry. Could this be a sign for him and his future? Only time will tell. Also, at this point, I have to tell you of another miracle, that of Janet, after six years of Anorexia, becoming a Mum three times over in the subsequent births of Sarah, Emma and Laura! Praise the Lord! Before leaving the subject of depression, there are two things that any past, present or future depressive should always remember; never to get overtired and never to get into a situation from which there is no escape; neither of which is easy to do, but both of which we ignore at our peril!

It is because all that has happened is now a real and lasting part of what I am, that I now feel able to go on to talk about my ministry and particularly that part of it which since 1988 has been at the very heart of it, namely as an Honorary Chaplain to St.Catherine's Hospice, Lostock Hall, Nr.Preston.

The Hospice, the basic part of which dates from the 19th Century and stands in its own grounds, was originally a country house and later a convalescent home, before undergoing a great deal of restoration work to open its door in its present capacity in 1985. It broadly serves the area of Preston, Chorley and South Ribble, in caring for those suffering mainly from Cancer, but also from other illnesses as well, such as Motor Neurones Disease, Multiple Sclerosis and Cerebral Palsy; also in giving support to families, in what for all of them is a very traumatic time during which they are seeking to come to terms with all that is happening to loved ones and, each in their own way, endeavouring to find answers to many seemingly unanswered questions.

The Hospice's main aim, in keeping with Hospice Philosophy as a whole, is to provide the highest quality of life for every patient in view of their condition and is seen essentially as a resource for life and living, rather than as a place where people come to die. As such, patients come to us for a variety of reasons; pain and symptom control, respite care so that carers or families can have a rest or a holiday, or because the patient's condition is becoming more serious and in need of prolonged nursing care, when the Hospice serves as a half-way house to entering a nursing home. Or again, they come to St.Catherine's because they are reaching the end of their earthly journey and need to be surrounded by 24 hour skilled and tender loving care, that not only gives to the patient a real sense of security, but also provides relief for the family as well, in that it removes a lot of responsibility and allows them to visit for as long and as often as they wish, day or night, without having to worry about the practical requirements of care such as feeding, lifting, toileting, washing and so on, unless of course they express a wish to be involved, in which case there is no problem, except that the individual needs and condition of patients may need them to be open to supervision by the nursing staff. Frank Allison, a family friend, summed up the care he received in the Hospice as " like being held in a hammock of love;" and during my long connection there, I have heard countless similar or even more magnanimous expressions of appreciation from patients and families both for the care and the very special people who provide it, be it as in-patients, day-patients, or in their own homes. In addition to nursing care, which also includes physiotherapy, there are also facilities for Aromatherapy, Reflexology, Chiropody, Hairdressing, Hand-care and gentle massage. The day care unit, which caters for twenty patients per day and balances up with the twenty in-patient beds, also has a dedicated staff, and in addition to caring for patients medical needs, also encourages hobbies and the development of artistic gifts which so many of the patients have. Social workers are also on hand to help wherever possible, with such things as negotiations for state grants, for home visits to assess the practicability of patients returning to their own home and what help in the form of a care package they will need to do so; or should this not be feasible to arrange visits to nursing / rest homes for the patients with their families. The need for the Spiritual care of patients and their families, without the infringement of privacy or confidentiality, is recognised as a real and necessary part of Hospice life and is undertaken by the Hospice Chaplain, with the assistance of an inter-denominational team of honorary chaplains. This is broadly what the Hospice provides and together with the links with the Ribblesdale Unit at Royal Preston Hospital and Chorley and District Hospital, now ensures that patients have complete palliative and pastoral care from the moment of diagnosis throughout their illnesses.

My involvement with St.Catherine's began approximately two and a half years after its opening when I visited Frank Allison, a long time friend whom I have already referred to for his description of the hospice as "a hammock of love". While I was there, an emergency arose with another patient and I was asked to help which I readily did and then visited the remainder of the patients at that time before leaving. Prior to this, whenever I had passed the end of the driveway to St.Catherine's, I had often wondered, as no doubt many had done before me and many have done so since, what was happening inside. Now I had an insight and thinking back, it would be true to say that I felt drawn towards a real involvement right from the first time I walked through the door. I continued to visit Frank fairly regularly and eventually, when other commitments eased, I asked to see the then Matron, Miss Elizabeth Swarbrick, to discuss the possibility of daily visits to all in-patients. She was delighted with what she saw as an answer to prayer, but first it was necessary for the matter to be discussed with the Rev. Tom Barnes, then Vicar of the Parish of St.Saviour Bamber Bridge, who, because St.Catherine's lies within the parish boundaries, held the title of Honorary Chaplain from the diocese. As a busy Parish Priest Tom naturally had no objections to a helping hand, and together with the clergy from St.Mary's Roman Catholic Church and the

Minister from the Methodist Church, both in Bamber Bridge, the Chaplaincy team was now operational.

How then, do I see the overall purpose of the Hospice and my role within it? Well, you may recall that at the beginning of Chapter Two, I made reference to my time in South India and to the small whitewashed church that we passed regularly on the journey to work. It is not remembered for any architectural feature, but rather for the notice in the small window above the main door which read, 'Come apart and rest awhile', and I refer to it again now, because these are the words that I would put over the door of St.Catherine's or indeed of any other hospice; as an invitation to those who are bearing the heat and burden of the day, not in foreign climes, but in serious illness, in pain, suffering or bereavement, to 'come apart and rest awhile', before continuing their journeys, some back to home and family, some to rest or nursing homes, some to their eternal home in heaven; and to their loved ones as they face a new phase in their lives, in trying to come to terms with life without the physical presence of the one who, in his or her unique way has touched, and been, so much a part of their life. Which is why I have a problem when I hear people talk in terms of 'terminal' illness. In no way can I think of the hospice as a terminus, the end of the road, a place patients come to die, but rather, as I said earlier, a resource centre for life and for living, a place of loving care and concern which will prepare and equip them for the next stage of their journey wherever it may lead them; which is why I for one was delighted when the hospice logo was changed from that of two hands in prayer surrounding the hospice, to two hands in prayer releasing the butterfly, to symbolise the on-going life, first surrounded and cared for and then released with tender loving care.

The word Priest is derived from the latin word pontifex which means a bridge builder, and this is basically how I see ministry or pastoral and spiritual care as a whole, building bridges, and it is this thought which lies at the very heart of everything I say and do in St.Catherine's and anywhere else for that matter.

The first video produced for the hospice had as its title, 'Being there', and it underlines what I see as the first basic requirement of hospice pastoral and spiritual care; to be there, maybe to say nothing or do nothing as the need dictates, but to be there, a physical presence which somehow speaks of deeper things and of a love, care and concern through and beyond that of nursing and the control of pain. And, in order to help make that love, care and concern a living reality for the patient, the second basic requirement of physical contact is, in my view, wherever possible, an essential element of care. To hold hands, to stroke the hand, the arm, or the forehead if the patient is sleepy or semi-conscious, often with quiet words of reassurance, or even with no words at all, can and does so often mean so much, not only for the patients but also for their families as well.

Some time ago now, many of you would have seen the T.V. programme about the late Princess Diana in Angola with those who had lost limbs or suffered other dreadful injuries due to land mines, and although many things have been said about her, and not always complimentary, one thing is sure, she possessed without doubt, the wonderful and precious gift of communication and bridge building, in the way she looked and touched and expressed her deepest feelings, often without words, to those to whom in a very real sense she was ministering 'healing.' I was privileged to witness this gift at first hand when Princess Diana came to open a new extension at St.Catherine's on 13th January 1993. From the T.V. programme you may also have noted something else which is very important, namely that her body posture got her down to where people were. She would sit alongside them, or kneel beside them, she didn't stand over them to overpower or overawe them; and these are things that I have always felt to be important, because it is vital that no patient should feel threatened in any way. Which in turn is why it is important not to offend in what we do. For whilst putting an arm around a patient or giving them a hug are both recommended as being good therapeutically, and therefore are attitudes and actions that one has to feel free to adopt as the situation allows, extreme care must be taken in order to avoid the risk of seeming over familiar, particularly in the early stages of a relationship with a patient or with a member of his or her family, having always in mind their right to privacy at all times. This right is of great importance, so much so that at times, 'being there' can also mean 'being readily available if required,' and possibly nothing more; this being the case, it has to be respected.

During my years in St.Catherine's we have had a fairly wide spectrum of patients including Atheists, Agnostics, Jehovah's Witnesses, Christadelphians, nominal or four-wheeled Christians, dedicated and practising Christians of all denominations including Greek Orthodox, together with Muslims, Hindus, Buddhists and Jews. Consequently, one has to be very sensitive to individual needs and to the religious requirements of the different religions and cultures involved, and to endeavour not to give any cause for embarrassment or offence to others, or on the other hand, not to feel in any way offended or rejected if the patient or his or her family exercise their right of privacy in requesting no visits from the Chaplain, thank you! Then again, 'being there' or 'being available' also involves the need for an introduction, which, in the main, only need be short. For example, "hello Margaret, I'm Alan, one of the Chaplaincy team; I come into the hospice four evenings a week to visit all the patients and to help wherever I can." It need be no more than that, but often it leads to further questions such as "Where is your church?" "What denomination do you belong to?" "Are you a priest, or a vicar or a minister?" "What do we call you?" I usually say in answer to the latter, "just call me what you like, whatever feels right to you is alright to me, I answer to anything even hey, you!"

Once introductions are made and I have given them a little outline of our side of the work, with the majority of patients it is a case of being a good listener, not only to give the patient confidence and to allow them to feel at home in being able to talk freely, but also to let them see that you are showing a real interest in them, their background, their family, their work, and how they have arrived at where they are at that moment of time, with the occasional question to help them in sharing what is so very important to them. Very often, they will also tell you how they stand spiritually, belief wise and church wise; and all the time, one is able to begin to build up a picture that can be used effectively in times of prayer together, if these materialise: which is why, after having listened carefully and attentively to all that they have had to say, I have to decide whether to wait, or to ask there and then, if they would like me to say a prayer for them and for the family, and one must never presume that the answer will be yes. Should they decline, it could be for a variety of reasons. It could be that they have no time for prayer and no belief in it, or on the other hand it could be that they have not said their prayers for such a long time that they feel awkward or embarrassed, or perhaps hypocritical in doing so now because they are in real need!

Whenever there is a negative response, for whatever reason, I always assure the patient concerned that I fully respect what they are saying to me, as will the rest of the team as well, but at the same time I do ask them to promise that if ever they feel the need of prayer, they will not hesitate to tell us. In other words, even though they don't wish to have prayer, we still care, they are still a real part of the family and we will still call in to see them; I also say a prayer for them in the Hospice chapel before leaving for home.

In the case of Jehovah's Witnesses, it is always understood that they do not wish to have any prayers said with them, other than by their own members or leaders, but there have been exceptions. The same is also true of Christadelphians, but not so strictly, whereas in the case of Muslims, Hindus and Buddhists, I have found them most gracious towards, and welcoming of prayers, and often requesting them. One patient who comes readily to mind is Fiaz, a Muslim gentleman who was married to an English lady by the name of Pearl and together they had a delightful family. Right from our first meeting it was Fiaz's wish that I say prayers with him, and there were many times also when the family were present and readily joined in. His brother was a devout Muslim and many times during the day, he could be found on his knees in the chapel facing towards Mecca, saying his prayers. One day, I took in a prayer mat, which I had been given many years before by a neighbour, and laid it out for him in his corner, but of course made no mention of it to him. The next time I saw him, he was so excited, "it was you, wasn't it!" "What was me, what are you blaming me for now?" "It was you who put out the prayer mat for me!" His eyes filled with tears and I was left with no option, I had to confess, and I had a friend for life. Whenever a Muslim dies, there are many rituals to be observed before the body is taken on its final journey, in this case to Pakistan, and I was very moved when the family asked me to say a final prayer for Fiaz before his body left the hospice; he had become a very dear friend whom I will never forget and from whom I learned a great deal; I hope that the same was true for him.

The importance of prayer in the hospice situation cannot be over emphasized, and in St.Catherine's it is a real part of everyday life, but always respecting patients' wishes. So what do I see as the fundamental principles involved in praying with individual patients? We have already thought about the importance of 'being there', and of the willing ear for as long as it takes; they are basic to everything in that the hopes, the fears, the frustrations and many other sorts of emotions being felt by the patient at this moment of time in their life, rise to the surface and are expressed by them to the best of their ability. And here, it also has to be said, that one should be very honest and forthright with the patient or relative in responding to questions they may ask in the process, taking care not to be drawn on any medical or nursing matter that may be broached, as this could lead to serious problems. It is also important, wherever possible, to share one's own experiences with patients and / or relatives, because one can then show real empathy which in most cases is readily identified and taken on board; and not to forget that a good sense of humour on both sides can also help a great deal at difficult moments, as a real bonus to all concerned. Like the lady patient who was asked by her daughter to help her to prepare for her driving test the following day. It was only a one- part test at that time and little by little they were working through the Highway Code. They had reached the part concerning junctions and particularly the ones marked off in yellow boxes with the instruction 'do not enter the box unless your exit is clear'. At this point the patient began to laugh out loud and her daughter asked her what it was all about. "Well, it's your driving test, but I think this instruction is just as important for me on my journey as it will be for you on yours!!"

Let me now turn your thoughts to some of the main difficulties with which one has to cope in prayer as a consequence of what has been revealed in conversation.

First there is the problem of the patient feeling worthless and useless. So many patients need to be assured of their worth before God and of how precious they are in His sight, and that even though they may not have had much time for Him in the past, His love for them has never changed. He gave them life and He sent His Son into the world to tell them and all of us of His love for us, His forgiveness of our sins, His power to heal, and to die for us, so that we might have His precious gift to us of eternal life. Patients need to hear this blessed assurance, and prayer is one of the precious vehicles through which it can be accomplished in sharing with the patient and his or her family, the wonder of God's loving care and concern for them, both individually and collectively. One is also able to incorporate thoughts from the scriptures to support and reassure them. For example from the 23rd, 121st and 139th Psalms, the parable of the Lost Sheep (St.Matthew chapter 18,verses 12-14), and our Lord's references to the sparrows and the hairs of our heads all being numbered (St Matthew chapter 10, verses 29-31).

Secondly, there is so often the need for patients to rediscover for themselves a sense of usefulness and purpose in lives that, quite understandably from their point of view, seem aimless and useless. "What good am I to anyone anymore?" "What can I do in this condition which is really worthwhile?" Just two of many such remarks, often accompanied by tears to emphasize and underline how deeply those who make them are feeling their dilemma. It is here that the value of prayer is again to be seen, this time as therapy of real purpose, not only in my prayers for them, but also in their prayers for themselves and for others. For no matter how limited they may be and feel in the physical sense, in the main their capacity to pray for themselves, their families, their fellow patients, for the staff who care for them, and for those whose generosity made the hospice possible in the first place and whose continued support provides for the running of it day to day, is enormous. (There may of course be some restriction here in the case of those with brain tumours or suffering from acute depression as a result of their condition.) So often, the offering of this positive side of prayerful participation has given new purpose and a new sense of fulfilment to those who hitherto have felt themselves to be useless. Furthermore, I firmly believe that the prayers of those who are themselves sharing in the sufferings of Jesus have a special effectiveness, in that they are being offered, humbly and sincerely, from hearts nearer to Him and to His will than ours, and that for many, the prayers offered in times of personal pain, discomfort and weariness are of real and lasting worth, and so very often achieve far more than has been achieved in health and at the height of physical power and ability, when without moving one inch, or even batting an eyelid, they have in prayer reached outwards and upwards to the very throne of God Himself.

Thirdly, very often patients also need support in prayer when they question their own worth and usefulness to their families. They need to be reassured that they are very precious indeed to their loved ones and not a burden to them, and that furthermore the family's ability to cope, now and in the future, is so often dependant on the way in which they see them coping now. This is not to place an added burden on the patient, but to emphasize that they are still a real part of the family and that what they say and do still matters so much! All of which, underlines how important it is for each and every one of us to make the most of every day, and to use whatever time we have, to say the things we need to say and to do the things we need to do; in trying our best to sort out any problems or difficulties which may exist between us, and to be understanding and ready to forgive.

The fourth type of situation comes when patients are afraid of what lies before them, not necessarily of death, because the vast majority have come in their own way to be reconciled with it and will talk freely about it, but rather in the way that it will happen. Obviously at this stage much will depend on the strength or otherwise of their personal faith, but in the main they need to be reassured of God's love for them and that in Jesus they have someone who knows all about it; one who has been through it all Himself, who understands exactly how they feel and who says to them personally, "don't be anxious, trust me and remember I am with you always, every moment, every step of the way." Over the years I have also found the words of hymns especially helpful, as no doubt you have already guessed from what has gone before, and in this particular instance those of Bishop W.Walsham How,

O my Saviour, lifted
From the earth for me,
Draw me, in thy mercy,
Nearer unto thee.

Lift my earth-bound longings,
Fix them, Lord, above;
Draw me with the magnet
Of thy mighty love.

Lord, thine arms are stretching
Ever far and wide,
To enfold thy children
To thy loving side.

And I come, O Jesus:
Dare I turn away?
No, thy love hath conquered,
And I come to-day;

Bringing all my burdens,
Sorrow, sin, and care,
At thy feet I lay them,
And I leave them there.

A fifth source of need is identified in those who feel that they have left it all too late! Earlier, when I was talking about patients willingness or otherwise to have prayers said for them, there will always be those who feel that to burden Jesus with their problems at this time is hypocritical and especially so if they have had little or no time for Him in the past. They need to be reassured that even though they may have fallen short in their relationship in the past, and that even though they may well think that it is hypocritical to call on Him now, the love of Jesus is so great that it is never too late to come to Him; and no cry for help ever goes unheeded. "Whoever comes to me, I will never turn them away," says Jesus; (St.John, chapter 6 verse 37) as the penitent thief on the cross next to Jesus discovered for himself, and you can't leave it much later than that! But how much better to do something about it now, rather than to leave everything to chance and to that next opportunity which may well never present itself!

The sixth and final source of need comes in dealing with the very real issues of mourning and preparation for death; and here you may be thinking that I have got them in the wrong order, but I don't think so. You see, so often we think of mourning and bereavement in terms of the relatives and friends of the deceased, and in St Catherine's we have facilities for that purpose in the form of a bereavement group, St.Catherine's Wheel; but we tend to forget, or perhaps up to now we have not even realised, that the mourning process applies just as much, if not moreso, to patients themselves. For whilst relatives and friends will have to cope with the loss of a loved one, the loved one is having to cope with the leaving behind of many loved ones, and this is happening now!

Some patients choose to cope with their bereavement in isolation, they switch off, they do not want to know, they just want to get on with the process of dying, while there are others, by far the vast majority, who are very positive and busy themselves in getting all their affairs sorted out so that their loved ones will have the weight of this taken from their shoulders when the time comes. There are also those who are concerned to sort out every detail of their funeral so that it may bring comfort and reassurance to those they are leaving behind, and in so doing are themselves comforted in their own time of bereavement. The practical side of getting things in order, however, may not always be sufficient, and pastorally and spiritually it may be necessary to go deeper. There are not many plusses so far as cancer and other patients may be concerned, but one plus is that in most instances, they do have time, very limited though in many cases this is, to put things right, to say what needs to be said, and to do what needs to be done. Often there is the matter of sorting out relationships that have gone wrong, and the healing of hurts often long standing over many years, sometimes involving relatives, sometimes friends, where there is a deep need for reconciliation and peace of mind. There is also for all of us the need to make our peace with God as well as with each other, and this can often mean dealing with consciences heavy with thoughts of past transgressions and deep feelings of guilt. Sometimes the load is so great that it has to be dealt with by way of confession and absolution, the Sacrament of Penance, and a rededication of one's whole being to God; which in one particular instance was followed by Holy Baptism. It has always been a great privilege to be part of this healing process and to see at first hand the tremendous relief experienced by the patient and the deep peace that ensued, not only for the patient but also for the family as well.

One example of this was in the case of Don and Janet. Don had been a fighter pilot in the United States Air Force; having seen active service he had a lot of memories of that time, some that he treasured and some that he would rather have forgotten. Janet, a schoolteacher, was much younger and when Don's condition worsened she stayed at home to care for him. When he came to us, we spent a lot of time talking about life in general, about his illness and how he saw his faith in relation to it, about their life together and what difference his illness had made to that life; we also spent a lot of time praying together. Although Janet always put on a brave face, there was no doubt in my mind that she was struggling at times to hold it all together for Don's sake, whilst he, for his part, appeared to be coping but with reservations. One day I expressed my thoughts to Janet, who said that she too had felt the same about him, and together we were of the opinion that I needed to spend time alone with Don and to search at a deeper level for a solution for him. A little time later, Don and I were alone and I happened to say how wonderful it would be if we could all make a new start in life and right the many things that we are not happy with. "It certainly would" he replied, and his eyes opened wide with excitement, or was it eager expectation? During the time he had been with us in the hospice, Don and I had developed a good and trusting relationship; I knew that he was a lapsed Roman Catholic but even so I did not want to cause him any more problems than he already had. I assured him that the new start he longed for was awaiting him; the question was whether he wanted me to help him or to arrange for him to see the Roman Catholic chaplain? There was no hesitation; he wanted me. For obvious reasons I cannot give you details, suffice it to say that he opened his heart to God and committed the rest of his life to Him; and with the benefit of Absolution he began his new life in Christ with that inner peace which passes all understanding. Again it was lovely to see and to share in the transformation, not only in Don but in Janet as well, and together we gave thanks in prayer. A matter of days later with all obstacles removed, Don passed peacefully into the kindlier world and since then for Janet there has been a time which has seen her pass through bereavement, yes with sadness in the loss from this world of the husband she loved and still loves very much, but also with a new found faith which has led her to the final stages of her preparation as a Methodist Local Preacher, with a view to progressing in due course to full-time ministry. When we talked and prayed together in St.Catherine's, we little thought that such a rich harvest was in store. "Praise the Lord!"

While on the subject of prayer for patients as part of the healing process, I want to underline its importance for families as well and to say that wherever possible they are encouraged to be part of it, in joining hands in a circle of prayer which speaks of eternal life and of God's unending and unbreakable love for us all; while our prayers at all times need to be positive, in asking that God will give to the patient and to the family, the assurance of the promise of Jesus to be with them always, that He will give their loved one freedom from pain and discomfort, deep and refreshing sleep and that healing which comes from His hands alone, and to the family all things needful for them at that time and in the days ahead, and that God will keep them all in His peace, surround them with His love, and support them and enfold them in His everlasting and ever-loving arms, now and always. It has been my experience that to pray in this way is very precious for all concerned, in that, on the one hand it helps the patient to feel more at ease in the knowledge that both he/she and the family are in God's care and under His guidance and protection, and on the other hand, it helps to strengthen the bond between patient and family, and helps the latter to feel that they have made a positive contribution to the situation, whereas previously they had perhaps felt inadequate and overwhelmed by it all and powerless to help.

Throughout my ministry I have always prayed for healing and the hospice situation is no exception, although for many, including some clergy, this is not easy to cope with, when on the one hand they want to give encouragement and reassurance, but on the other hand find the situation difficult to handle if no visible improvement takes place or the patient dies; which in turn may also explain why, in comparison with the number of patients we have had over the years, visits from clergy other than the Chaplaincy team have been very few indeed. Having said this, one has to acknowledge that it is not the easiest part of ministering to the sick, and I must confess that every time I am going up the main driveway to visit in the hospice I pray for help and guidance, and to be given the right words for any situation that may be awaiting me. But regarding the need to pray for healing I am in no doubt, because my reason for being in the hospice in the first place is because I believe that all those who work there, and who give so much love and care in easing the physical pain and in giving of themselves and their nursing and medical skills, do so basically, in terms of the here and now, while it is in the sphere of pastoral and spiritual care, that we as chaplains not only embrace fully the here and now, but also reach out from here to eternity. So that, as I see it, prayers for healing are inextricably linked to and demanded by our Christian faith and belief in the unfailing love of God and the resurrection to eternal life, in and through our Lord Jesus Christ, and as such are an essential part of that blessed assurance that all of us need to have.

The longing to be healed must be the one uppermost in the minds of all who are ill, not least in cancer sufferers, and it is one that is aggravated more and more in those cases where the human body is visibly wasting away, or where the presence of a brain tumour is gradually closing down the body's functions, which broadly is also the case with the increasing paralysis caused by Motor Neurones Disease, (M.N.D); both of which patients and families find it increasingly difficult to cope with, particularly with the intense and rapid loss of body weight; which is why I believe it so important to maintain and underpin the longing to be healed, not only in order to lift patients and families out of despair, or to be kind, or to lull them into a sense of security, but because healing is God's will for them. "I am the Lord, who heals you" (Exodus chapter 15 verse 26), "Praise the Lord O my soul; all my inmost being, praise his holy name. Praise the Lord, O my soul, and forget not all his benefits - who forgives all your sins and heals all your diseases" (Psalm 103, verses 1-3). Such thoughts are also reflected in St.John chapter 3 verse 16,"For God so loved the world that he gave his one and only Son, that whoever believes in him shall not perish but have eternal life." Then again, when St John in his gospel refers to the miracles of Jesus, he calls them "signs", coming from the Greek word 'Arrabon', which also means, the earnest, the guarantee of something which is yet to be. Could it be that this something is what we find in the Book of Revelation, when in chapter 21 verse 5, John tells how God speaking to him about what must be hereafter, says, " I am making everything new!" Then he said, "Write this down, for these words are trustworthy and true"? Are we then, to see the healings of Jesus, then and now, whether it may be in my healing from depression or the many cancer sufferers who go into remission, as the earnests, the guarantees that enable us to look forward with confidence and thanksgiving to the most perfect healing of all in heaven? "Behold I am making everything new", such that whether healing takes place here or in eternity does not alter the fact that our prayers for healing are heard and that the answer to them will be the best for all concerned. Yes, it is only natural that we cling to what we know and what we have experienced so far, but as Christians we must not be earthbound, "For here we do not have an enduring city, but we are looking for the city that is to come" (Hebrews chapter 13 verse 14). We must look to Jesus and to life in Him in unbroken continuity, in this life and through the moment of death into His nearer presence in eternity, in our Heavenly Father's house with its many rooms that St John tells us about in chapter 14 verses 1-6 of his gospel; knowing as St Paul writes in Romans chapter 8 verses 38-39, that, "neither death nor life, neither angels nor demons, neither the present nor the future, nor any powers, neither height nor depth, nor anything else in all creation, will be able to separate us from the love of God that is in Christ Jesus our Lord," and that as Paul reminds the Corinthians in his first letter to them chapter 2 verse 9 "No eye has seen, no ear has heard, no mind has conceived, what God has prepared for those who love him."

Soon after I was ordained, I visited the Rev William Brandwood - then Vicar of St.Leonard's Church - in hospital, where he was suffering from cancer; and I will never forget one of the things he said to me.

"I could not have gone through all this if I hadn't known that Jesus had been through it all before me and that He is with me now." And he was so right, Jesus does know all about the pain, the anger, the frustration, the embarrassment, the bitterness, the resentment, the anxiety and care for loved ones and the many other emotions we experience in life, and he understands, he cares and he wants to share. "Here I am! I stand at the door and knock. If anyone hears my voice and opens the door, I will come in and eat with him and he with me." (Revelation chapter 3 verse 20) It is in saying 'yes' to Jesus that we not only come to discover what He means when He says, "behold, I am with you always," but also the answer to our deepest needs; which is why the deep desire to make this known to those in our care, so that it may become a living reality for them in their hour of need, lies at the very heart of my ministry to patients and their families. For there is no doubt that a commitment or re-dedication of one's life to Jesus, not only enables us to find fulfilment in the rest of our lives here on earth, but also to look forward with confidence and anticipation to sharing with Jesus and all our loved ones, in the peace and joy and healing of heaven.

In the Hospice we not only minister to our patients prayerfully, but also Sacramentally as well in Holy Communion and Holy Unction (Anointing); having already mentioned the one or two occasions when Holy Baptism has also been administered, and the Sacrament of Penance (Confession and Absolution) as requested. There are normally two celebrations of Holy Communion each week, one for Church of England and Free Church day and in-patients, and the other for our Roman Catholic patients. Where patients are unable to attend chapel, but still desire to receive the Blessed Sacrament, there is no problem in taking it to them in their room or rooms after the service, and in cases where patients have been used to receiving more regularly, arrangements are made for them to continue to do so. When patients receive the Sacrament by their bedside and members of the family are present, wherever possible with the patient's permission, I invite them to join with us in what is a very precious time, because I believe with all my heart that in this wonderful Sacrament of Holy Communion we have been given the bridge between here and eternity, where we are one with Jesus, the angels and archangels and all the company of Heaven, and that Jesus, in giving Himself to us, brings with Him all who are with Him now, so that we are one with Him and with each other at the meeting point of time and eternity in which death is no more. Here there is comfort and reassurance for us all; here there is the certainty and reality of one unbroken fellowship in Christ Jesus our Lord, which death may threaten but cannot overcome. This is a thought from which families themselves have also found great comfort in dealing with their bereavement, in the knowledge that in the moment of Holy Communion, they too can rediscover for themselves the joy of Easter morning!!

In the letter of James, chapter 5 verses 13-15, we read, "Is any one of you in trouble? He should pray. Is anyone happy? Let him sing songs of praise. Is any one of you sick? He should call the elders of the church to pray over him and anoint him with oil in the name of the Lord. And the prayer offered in faith will make the sick person well; the Lord will raise him up. If he has sinned he will be forgiven."

For centuries in the Roman Catholic Church the Sacrament of Unction or Extreme Unction, has been seen as a preparation for death; as a result of which it has been used more widely and more frequently by the Roman Catholic Church, than by the Church of England and the Anglican Church in general, where it is seen primarily as a Sacrament of Healing; which is how

I see its use in the hospice. At the same time, there has also been a change of heart in the Roman Catholic Church as well, where in the main it is now referred to as the Sacrament of the Sick. But unfortunately for older patients the association with 'the Last Rites' still remains and they can often become quite upset; which is why there is a real necessity to be sensitive and to make sure that as far as possible both patients and their families are fully aware of what this Sacrament is all about and are fully in agreement with its being administered. Done in this way, the results are very satisfying indeed for all concerned.

For those whose earthly part of their journey comes to an end in the hospice, their passing into 'the kindlier world,' is surrounded by prayers for them and for their families; prayers of thanksgiving for his or her life and the commendation of that life to Almighty God; prayers too for comfort, guidance and reassurance for the family in their hour of need and in the days ahead, when each of them in their own way will be doing their best to come to terms with life without the physical presence of the one , who in their own very special and unique way has touched the lives of them all and more besides. We of the Chaplaincy are also there to give any help and guidance we can to the family to ease the initial shock and burden, and over the years I have been asked many times, either by patients or their families, to officiate at funerals. In fact there are many families I still visit from time to time to let them know that they are not forgotten.

Any summary of ministry in the hospice would be incomplete without reference to the extension of pastoral and spiritual care to the staff and their families; it's the same old story, 'who cares for the carers'? There is no doubt that the pressures on the nursing staff are great and the tender loving care they give, which involves so much the giving of themselves, takes its toll, not only physically but also mentally and spiritually as well, as they share with patients in their daily pilgrimage and all that is involved. As a result, they too have problems with the strain and weariness of it all, and as such they too need help and encouragement to support them and to help them to recharge their batteries. There was also a period of two years when there were an extraordinary number of bereavements suffered by members of staff themselves not to mention hospitalisation for a number of them; all in all a rather harrowing time for all concerned!

I hope and pray that these thoughts we have shared will not only give you a real insight into what we are seeking to do in our part of the Lord's vineyard, but will also be of help to you if and when you are called upon to deal with similar situations; that by God's grace and help, we may all be the willing channels of His love and healing power in the world to those in need.

I leave you with this story for your encouragement.

John in many ways was representative of many of our patients. When I first met him he was very cheerful and welcoming, but didn't take long to tell me that he had no real faith and no church background; his only connection with any church being that he had sign-written the notice board outside St.George's Church in Chorley! Well, it was a start, and at times one has to be thankful for small mercies, and during the visits that followed we talked about his life as a whole and within it, his family and his work; and little by little I moved nearer to asking him whether he would like me to say a prayer for him and his family. Had I just asked to pray for John himself, I think he would have declined the offer, and just why I included the family at that point I don't know, although in retrospect I realise the Lord did! John was clearly moved, and from then on we asked for help and guidance for them all.

Eventually he was discharged and returned home to his family, and I heard no more of him, until I received a short note on a scrap of paper; which I still have and will always treasure; it is a message from Jennie, one of our Home Care Team which says, "John James died very peacefully last Sunday. He had made his peace with God, and wanted you to know how much you had helped him to do so."

Thank you John for your thoughtfulness and for your words that mean so much, for now, and for the future, in encouragement and inspiration.

CHAPTER SIX

Following my retirement from the brewery in 1985, which also meant an end to my three years as a relief chaplain in H.M. Prison Wymott, in itself a very interesting and often amusing experience; I served for a period as Assistant Chaplain in Sharoe Green Hospital, Preston, to Canon Eddie (We have a Gospel to proclaim) Burns. The work was located in the Gynaecological and Geriatric Units, both of which posed their own particular problems, which in turn called for understanding and sensitivity. It was in the former that I met a patient I will never forget and from whom I learned a great deal. We shared many precious thoughts and prayers and I know that it wasn't a case of one-way traffic, and that she too benefited from our meeting. As I walked up to her bed, I sensed a real aura of peace and tranquillity, and this became even more accentuated as we exchanged greetings; in other words, her voice and demeanour were such that the aura of peace and tranquillity was not only surrounding her, but was also within her, in her very being, such that I had to share with her what I was seeing, hearing and experiencing, whereupon she assured me that I was not mistaken, and that the thoughts I was sharing with her, had already been expressed by many other people previously. Greta was Polish, born and raised in a small village not far from Warsaw, where in time she had met, fallen in love with and married, her late husband. They had not been married very long when the Second World War started, and when the Germans subsequently invaded Poland they were arrested and sent to separate concentration camps. It was a terrible blow to them, as indeed it was to so many, and neither of them knew if they would ever meet again. At the end of hostilities and following liberation by the Allies, Greta, in a very poor way physically and mentally, did the only thing she could think of doing, and that was to make her way slowly and wearily, back to what was left of her native village, in the fervent hope that her husband, had he survived, would be doing the same. Her love and courage were rewarded, she arrived to find him already there; and so they began to pick up the pieces and to rebuild their life and their home, and eighteen months later their first child was born. It was not easy, but very much in love they triumphed over not a little adversity and enjoyed many happy years together with further increases in their family. But the privations of their captivity had taken their toll on them both, but particularly on her husband, and in the course of time he became critically ill and she recalled for me what happened on the morning of their last day together. It was Christmas Day, and as he lay unconscious with his hand in hers, her mind went from the confines of the sick room into the world outside where she thought about the millions of people excitedly opening the presents they had bought for each other. But what about Jesus, this was His birthday, how many will even be giving Him a thought, let alone a present? "It was then, that I decided what I had to do", she went on, "I would give Him my two most precious possessions, my husband and myself, and from the moment I did so, I was filled and surrounded by this wonderful peace and tranquillity that has never left me for one moment since. My family and friends were all mystified when they came to see me as to why I was so much in control of things and shedding no tears. It was only when I told them what I have told you that they began to realise, albeit only in part, what had happened, in that I was now experiencing for myself that peace of God that passes all human understanding and yet is so real and so precious as to be beyond measure and beyond words".

I have chosen the above story to introduce a thought that is very close to my heart, namely, that the Good News of Jesus and the essential difference He can and does make to those who freely and lovingly accept Him into their hearts and lives, is clear and simple and should wherever possible remain so. I remember reading at one time how Evelyn Underhill in her book 'Worship', defines worship as 'the response of the creature to the eternal,' and in the above story we see clearly and simply, the response of Greta to Jesus on His birthday in the form of her ready and loving gift of her husband's life and her own, in what we can readily call her act of worship and sacrifice to the One who is eternal, whom she has never seen, only heard about, and of whom up until now, she has had no personal experience. But now the scene is changed, her act of worship and sacrifice has been rewarded with the peace and tranquillity of the Divine presence within and around her; as a living reality that she has experienced ever since and which is just as real now as it ever was. It has transformed her life and is plain for all to see; it also carries with it, for those who know Greta, the longing to share it with her, so that in a nutshell we have here not only a personal experience and testimony, but also a spreading of the Good News, an evangelistic opportunity to be truly a disciple of Jesus, and a magnet and channel for His love and loving purposes in the world, and one can imagine Jesus using the story of Greta in the form of a parable to show clearly and simply what discipleship and the response to it is really all about.

I believe that the clear and simple approach is what the Church as a whole needs desperately to adopt in order to meet the demands of our world today, together with an emphasis on walking by faith and not by sight in the sense of ceasing to try to find academic answers to everything, thus reducing the power and majesty of Almighty God into understandable compartments, which ultimately for many, has meant a loss of faith even in the basic teachings of the Church. For example, in the Lancashire Evening Post of 22nd January 2003, we read, under the heading "It's a fact", "A survey has found that a third of Church of England clergy doubt or disbelieve in the physical Resurrection and only half are convinced of the truth of the Virgin Birth. And amongst the liberal clergy belief was much lower, with two-thirds expressing doubts in physical Resurrection and three-quarters unconvinced of the truth of the Virgin Birth. However, 75% accept the Doctrine of the Trinity and more than 80% are happy with the idea that God created the world." Well, even taking into consideration the fact that this particular newspaper does have a strong Roman Catholic bias, one has to admit that it all makes very depressing and to a great extent alarming reading, and together with the multiplicity of different denominations and teachings within the supposedly one Christian Church, can, and in many cases has resulted in a distinctly adverse effect upon its missionary enterprise. It also leaves the Church open to the charge of "Your God is too small and too confused" at a time of having to cope with the ever increasing multi-racial, multi-cultural and multi-faith society and the problems that arise from this, for the Church, for our nation and for the world, while at the same time having so often to walk the tight-rope of accusations of racial, cultural and religious discrimination. All of which emphasises the desperate need for the Christian Church as a whole to get its priorities and teachings in order and in so doing to be willing, in loving obedience to God, to lay aside the differences between its denominations, which in so many cases are man-made and motivated by selfishness and greed and in direct opposition to His will, as its act of sacrifice and worship for the furtherance of His kingdom.

Furthermore I believe that the clear and simple approach already referred to earlier, and which was the hallmark of the teaching and preaching of Jesus Himself, needs to be revived and re-established at the heart of our own teaching and preaching, and that the time has come for academics, theologians and writers not only to agree on a clear and simple statement of basic Christian principles and truths, as set out in the Word of God in Holy Scripture, but also on the best way forward to a clear and simple proclamation of God's word and the Good News of Jesus to the world in its hour of deepest need. Here, again I think we have a great deal to learn from music, and as shown earlier, from the words of hymns and songs which so often have the knack of stating profound truths in a simple and readily understood way. For example, there is no doubt that the number of books written on the subject of the Incarnation, the Coming of Jesus into the world 'Incarnatis', in the flesh, are legion, many of them seeing it in terms of what is known in 'the trade' as the Divine self-limitation, and all that that kind of terminology might mean for the academic mind but certainly not for the rest of us lesser mortals! But how many of these books, if any, have managed to express it so beautifully as Graham Kendrick in one of the verses of his truly inspiring hymn The Servant King, No 162 in Complete Mission Praise.

> Come see His hands and His feet,
> The scars that speak of sacrifice,
> Hands that flung stars into space,
> To cruel nails surrendered.

No, we may not be able to understand the thoughts of those who have sought honestly and sincerely to discover and to put into words what it all means, but we only need to focus our minds on this one verse of Graham Kendrick's hymn, the words of which he believes were given to him by God, to become lost in wonder, love and praise. Furthermore, we also come to realise the truth and wisdom in the words of Brother Tristam SSF, in his lovely book 'Exciting Holiness,' when, in speaking of Gregory of Nyssa, 330-394, he says,

> "For Gregory, God is met not as an object to be understood,
> but as a mystery to be loved."

Here I believe is not only an answer to the dilemma of those referred to above who find difficulty in accepting even basic teachings of the Church because they cannot fully understand or define them, but also a real encouragement to all of us to walk by faith and not by sight, and never to be afraid to acknowledge that we don't always have the answers, but nevertheless believe that what we offer in faith, will be blessed by God, both for those who give and those who receive. Thoughts very much reflected by the writer of Psalm 113, when in verses 3-8 we read,

The Lord's name is praised: from the rising up of the sun unto
the going down of the same.
The Lord is high above all heathen: and his glory above the
heavens.
Who is like unto the Lord our God, that hath his dwelling so high:
and yet humbleth himself to behold the things that are in heaven and
earth?
He taketh up the simple out of the dust: and lifteth up the poor out of
the mire; that he may set him with the princes: even with the princes
of his people.
He maketh the barren woman to keep house: and to be a joyful mother
of children.

(The Book of Common Prayer)

My initial plea for clarity and simplicity was in fact conditional; it was that 'wherever possible' this should be the case, as indeed it must be when it has to be acknowledged that it is one thing to meet the needs of the average church congregation, and another to meet the needs of those in theological colleges and universities. For while the basic needs of both are the same, the latter would be looking for stimulation on a more academic level than the former, even though the need to provide food for thought is a necessary requirement for both sets of hearers.

When Jesus appeared to the disciples in the upper room on the evening of Easter Day, two of them were missing; Thomas who had the nickname of 'Didymus' - the twin- and Judas Iscariot, who, when he realised what he had done in betraying Jesus to the authorities for thirty pieces of silver, was filled with remorse and as a result had gone out and hanged himself. When Thomas returned and the rest of the disciples told him what had happened, he said to them, "Unless I see the nail marks in his hands and put my finger where the nails were, and put my hand into his side, I will not believe it." A week later his disciples were in the house again, and Thomas was with them. Though the doors were locked, Jesus came and stood among them and said, "Peace be with you!" Then he said to Thomas, "Put your finger here; see my hands. Reach out our hand and put it into my side. Stop doubting and believe." We do not know if Thomas did in fact touch Jesus, all we know is what he said, "My Lord and my God!" Then Jesus told him, "because you have seen me, you have believed; blessed are those who have not seen and yet have believed." (St John Chapter 20 verses 24-29) At first glance it would appear that Jesus is stressing to Thomas that the important thing is to walk by faith and not by sight, but there is also another aspect to this story that is quite interesting and throws new light upon it. It revolves around Thomas's nickname of Didymus - the twin - but whose twin? Among the twelve disciples Jesus chose, there were two sets of brothers, Simon and Andrew, and James and John the two sons of Zebedee, but no mention of any other two-some let alone twin-some. But tradition from the early church has it that Thomas was so much like Jesus that they were like twins and were thought of as such by the rest. After the death of Jesus, Thomas was so distraught that he could not stay with the rest, but at risk to life and limb, for had he been caught, he would have suffered the same fate, he went out alone in order to find an answer, in order to sort out his mind; he had lost his alter - ego, his other self, the one in whom he had great faith and hope, it was a loss too great to bear. Consequently, when at last he felt able to rejoin the rest of them, and they began to tell him, "We have seen the Lord!" the last thing Thomas wanted or needed, was to have to go through all the pain and anguish again so soon after doing his best to cope with it in the first place; hence his reaction to what they told him, and his immediate response to Jesus when he saw Him, "my Lord and my God". Because Thomas was so near to Jesus and his personal faith in Him was so deep, and because we have no record of how the rest of the disciples responded to Jesus except that they were glad when they saw the Lord, but made no personal confessions of faith in Jesus as Thomas had done, it could well be that his words to Thomas about the importance of walking by faith and not by sight were meant more for the rest of the disciples then and now, rather than for Thomas himself; a source of food for thought for all of us.

Perhaps this is as good a time as any to think about our own situation and to ask how we have arrived there. For some of us it will be because of what we were taught about Jesus when we were children, at our mother's knee, in Day and Sunday School and in Church; when in so many ways although we could not see Him, He became real for us as a 'Friend for little Children', a friend we grew to love and to want to know more about; 'Tell me the stories of Jesus I long to hear' as the well-known children's hymn has it. As we have grown, so our thoughts have developed, and many of us will have tried to further our knowledge of Jesus in reading the Bible, perhaps with the help of the various Bible reading notes which are readily available and which provide daily readings accompanied by explanatory notes and often by prayers as well. There will also be those of us who, after an early start, in 'knowing' Jesus, have, for one reason or another, lost 'sight' of Him, possibly for a long time, only to have our thoughts turned to Him again in a time of trouble; when in sickness or in personal tragedy or bereavement, we don't know where to turn, when we need help, when so often we are looking for answers. On the other hand there will be some of us, who, having found ourselves in a personal wilderness, have sought to find our way 'home' in attending a Billy Graham Crusade meeting or something akin to it, and there, in hearing again the Good News of Jesus, have made or renewed our commitment to Him; which in turn has given us a new insight into things spiritual and a new determination to grow in what St.Paul calls, "attaining to the whole measure of the fullness of Christ." (Ephesians chapter 4 verse 13) There will also be some of us, who, because we have become so weighed down by guilt for something we have done, have in deep need, and even at times in desperation, thrown ourselves on the love and compassion of God in our search for forgiveness, restoration and peace; and so have begun a new life 'in Christ.' And so we could go on, the list is endless; all we can do is add our own experience to the list and hopefully and prayerfully, learn from the experiences of others.

No doubt the best example of spiritual growth and development we have in the New Testament is that of Saul of Tarsus, the arch-enemy and principal persecutor of the Church, who, through his conversion experience on the road to Damascus, became Paul the Apostle and the greatest ambassador for Christ the world has ever known. In his letter to the Philippians, chapter 3 verses 5-6, Paul lists his pre-Damascus Road credentials as "circumcised on the eighth day, of the people of Israel, of the tribe of Benjamin, a Hebrew of Hebrews; in regard to the law, a Pharisee; as for zeal, persecuting the church; as for legalistic righteousness faultless"; in other words, his credentials are impeccable; so that as he set out to Damascus with letters of authority from the High Priest to the synagogues there, to the effect that if he found any there who belonged to 'the Way'(one of the earliest titles for Christians), whether men or women, he might take them as prisoners to Jerusalem. In so doing Paul, or Saul as he then was, was convinced that he was acting completely in accordance with God's will and rendering Him faithful service. But events were to prove otherwise, for,"as he neared Damascus on his journey, suddenly a light from heaven flashed around him. He fell to the ground and heard a voice say to him, 'Saul, Saul, why do you persecute me?' 'Who are you, Lord?' Saul asked. 'I am Jesus, whom you are persecuting,' he replied, 'Now get up and go into the city and you will be told what you must do'" (Acts of the Apostles chapter 9, verses 1-6).

We may well wonder what thoughts were going through the mind of the hitherto confident Saul, now rendered blind and helpless; up to now his thoughts and intentions had been to rid the world of those of 'the Way', and now here he was talking to the One who was, and is, and always will be the Way, the Truth and the Life; in persecuting them, Saul was persecuting Him, they were His Body in the world! The fact that for three whole days he did not eat or drink anything has a lot to say about his state of mind and his physical blindness would also be reflected in his spiritual blindness as well! He was in turmoil, and it was only after he had been visited by Ananias, who, on entering the house, placed his hands on him and said, "Brother Saul, the Lord - Jesus, who appeared to you on the road as you were coming here - has sent me so that you may see again and be filled with the Holy Spirit," that things began to come clearer for him. " Immediately, something like scales fell from Saul's eyes, and he could see again. He got up and was baptised, and after taking some food, he regained his strength" (Acts chapter 9, verses 17-19), and it is in Philippians chapter 3,verses 7-11, that we see his transformation in mind and word from Saul of Tarsus, stalwart Jew and Pharisee to Paul the Apostle and servant of Jesus Christ, and what it meant to him. " Whatever was to my profit I now consider loss for the sake of Christ. What is more, I consider everything a loss compared to the surpassing greatness of knowing Christ Jesus my Lord, for whose sake I have lost all things. I consider them rubbish, so that I may gain Christ and be found in him, not having a righteousness of my own that comes from the law, but that which is through faith in Christ - the righteousness that comes from God and is by faith. I want to know Christ and the power of his resurrection and the fellowship of sharing in his sufferings, becoming like him in his death, and so, somehow, to attain to the resurrection from the dead." In saying this Paul is well aware that this is no easy matter, it requires from him a great deal of effort in rethinking his position and in working hard to make his new found faith in Jesus a living reality for himself before he can share it more effectively with others. "Not that I have already obtained all this, or have already been made perfect, but I press on to take hold of that for which Christ Jesus took hold of me. Brothers, I do not consider myself yet to have taken hold of it. But one thing I do: Forgetting what is behind and straining towards what is ahead, I press on towards the goal to win the prize for which God has called me heavenwards in Christ Jesus. All of us who are mature should take such a view of things. And if on some point you think differently, that too, God will make clear to you. Only let us live up to what we have already attained." (Philippians chapter 3.verses 12-16)

Paul's growth in his new-found faith was not without its problems and there were times when he did not have the same confidence that he had possessed in his pre-Damascus Road days. This is shown in his first letter to the Corinthians, where in chapter 2,verses 1-5 he shares with his readers just how he felt when he first visited them. "When I came to you, brothers, I did not come to you with eloquence or wisdom as I proclaimed to you the testimony about God. For I resolved to know nothing while I was with you except Jesus Christ and him crucified. I came to you in weakness and fear, and with much trembling. My message and my preaching were not with wise and persuasive words, but with a demonstration of the Spirit's power, so that your faith might not rest on men's wisdom, but on God's power."

As time went on, Paul gained in confidence and like Jesus was able to use the things around him, in order to press home religious truths and to encourage religious debate. This is seen very clearly in Paul's visit to Athens, where, after he has been preaching the good news of Jesus in the synagogue and in the market place to those who happened to be there, he was taken to task by a group of Epicurean and Stoic philosophers, who disputed what he had been saying and as a result took him and brought him to a meeting of the Areopagus, ('Mars hill', north-west of the Acropolis in Athens, from which the Council of the Areopagus which originally met there took its name), where they said to Paul, "May we know what this new teaching is that you are presenting? You are bringing some strange ideas to our ears, and we want to know what they mean." (All the Athenians and the foreigners who lived there spent their time in doing nothing but talking about and listening to the latest ideas.) Paul then stood up in the meeting of the Areopagus and said: "Men of Athens! I see that in every way you are very religious. For as I walked around and looked carefully at your objects of worship, (which had greatly distressed him) I even found an altar with this inscription: TO AN UNKNOWN GOD. Now what you worship as something unknown I am going to proclaim to you." So began his sermon, moving from creation to the resurrection of Jesus, in which he even quoted from their own poets in support of his argument.

"When they heard about the resurrection of the dead, some of them sneered, but others said, 'We want to hear you again on this subject'. At that, Paul left the Council. A few men became followers of Paul and believed. Among them was Dionysius, a member of the Areopagus, also a woman named Damaris, and a number of others" (Acts of the Apostles, chapter 17 verses 16-34).

So we see in Paul, someone who, although well established in life, was not afraid to let go and let God bring about a wonderful transformation in his life, from one self-confident to one solely dependant upon the power of God through the Holy Spirit, in what he said and did and underwent in his personal sufferings for the sake of the Gospel of Jesus. "Are they servants of Christ? (I am out of my mind to talk like this.) I am more. I have worked much harder, been in prison more frequently, been flogged more severely, and been exposed to death again and again. Five times I received from the Jews the forty lashes minus one. Three times I was beaten with rods, once I was stoned, three times I was shipwrecked, I spent a night and a day in the open sea, I have been constantly on the move. I have been in danger from rivers, in danger from bandits, in danger from my own countrymen, in danger from the Gentiles; in danger in the city, in danger in the country, in danger at sea; and in danger from false brothers. I have laboured and toiled and have often gone without sleep; I have known hunger and thirst and have often gone without food; I have been cold and naked. Besides everything else, I face daily the pressure of my concern for all the churches. Who is weak, and I do not feel weak? Who is led into sin, and I do not inwardly burn? If I must boast, I will boast of the things that show my weakness. The God and Father of the Lord Jesus, who is to be praised forever, knows that I am not lying"(2 Corinthians, chapter 11, verses 22-31).

Having given, or should we say boasted of his new credentials as a Christian, Paul is also very much aware of the danger of doing so, and so he underlines the fact that his boasting about his weakness is not to emphasize his own achievements, but rather to acknowledge how God's power is working in and through him. Furthermore, should he get carried away by getting so involved in his missionary work, as to forget this, he speaks openly about his thorn in the flesh which prevents him from doing so, "To keep me from becoming conceited, there was given me a thorn in my flesh, a messenger of Satan, to torment me. Three times I pleaded with the Lord to take it away from me. But he said to me, 'My grace is sufficient for you, for my power is made perfect in weakness.' Therefore I will boast all the more gladly about my weaknesses, so that Christ's power may rest on me. That is why, for Christ's sake, I delight in weaknesses, in insults, in hardships, in persecutions, in difficulties. For when I am weak, then I am strong" (2 Corinthians, chapter 12 verses 7-10). Just what his thorn in the flesh consisted of is not properly known, but it has been suggested that it could have been his poor eyesight or some other physical disability; it may also refer to periodic attacks of malaria involving blinding headaches to the extreme point of human endurance; or even to an individual person who was always acting as a devil's advocate. But whatever the nature or the cause, it was so hard to bear, that the normally 'hard-as- nails' Paul felt it necessary to ask the Lord to remove it from him, not once or twice, but on three occasions, only to be told, 'My grace is sufficient for you.' What these words meant for Paul we may never really know, for whilst in his missionary journeys, by land and sea, and throughout the rest of his life and ministry, he learned to lean very heavily on the Grace of God, it did not alter the fact that he had to endure 'his thorn' in addition to all the other hardships and privations which he encountered along the way. Is it any wonder, therefore, that at the end of his Letter to the Galatians he writes, "From henceforth let no man trouble me: for I bear in my body the marks of the Lord Jesus" (Chapter 6 verse 17 in the King James Version).

We cannot think about Paul the man, his work, his words and his sacrifice, without finding much food for thought, not only to support the need for clarity and simplicity in proclaiming the Good News of Jesus to others, but also to give us strength and courage to step out with determination, willing to take risks, even to the point of being thought of as 'fools for Christ's sake'; knowing without doubt that we can depend fully on the power of God through the Holy Spirit and that come what may, the Lord's Grace will be sufficient for us as it was for Paul, and that His strength will be made perfect in our weakness and our weaknesses.

We sing the glorious conquest
Before Damascus' gate,
When Saul, the Church's spoiler,
Came breathing threats and hate;
The ravening wolf rushed forward
Full early to the prey;
But lo! The shepherd met him,
And bound him fast to-day!

O Glory most excelling
That smote across his path!
O light that pierced and blinded
The zealot in his wrath!
O Voice that spake within him
The calm reproving word!
O love that sought and held him
The bondman of his Lord!

O wisdom, ordering all things
In order strong and sweet,
What nobler spoil was ever
Cast at the Victor's feet?
What wiser master-builder
E'er wrought at thine employ,
Than he, till now so furious
Thy building to destroy?

Lord, teach Thy Church the lesson,
Still in her darkest hour
Of weakness and of danger
To trust thy hidden power.
Thy grace by ways mysterious
The wrath of man can bind,
And in thy boldest foeman
Thy chosen saint can find.

Amen.

John Ellerton 1826-93.

CHAPTER SEVEN

During the period which followed my return from India in 1961 until beginning theological college in 1965, I returned to the Leyland Motors parent company where, after working on the India section which as the name suggests was responsible for all things appertaining to the factory in Madras from which I had just returned, I then became Overseas Liaison Engineer (Production), with responsibilities in two directions. First of all as Adviser on Planning and Production to the Government of India at their Heavy Vehicles Factory at Avadi, Madras, and secondly to E.N.A.S.A. (Empresa Nacional de Autocamiones S.A.) in Spain, with factories in Madrid and Barcelona. Both situations concerned the manufacture of Leyland engines under licence, the former, the L60 engine for use in a military vehicle, for which Self-Changing Gears of Coventry were responsible for the gearbox and transmission, and Vickers Armstrong of Newcastle were responsible for the hull; the latter various sizes of diesel engines for buses and trucks.

I have given you these details in order to explain how I came to be in the situations that resulted in the incidents I want to relate to you.

In my dealings with the Heavy Vehicles Factory at Avadi, which had been the site of a British Air Force base during the second world war and which was situated approximately 15 miles to the south of Madras, there was obviously a mountain of paper work to be sorted out and machines and equipment to be ordered, much of which was handled by the existing India section mentioned above, together with visits from the various personnel from the factory who came over for tuition and familiarisation with the product. Then came the time for me to go over, with another colleague, to spend three months at the factory, where we were housed in a compound nearby in a series of 'cells' which, although new, were fairly primitive to say the least, with a minimum of furniture for personal comforts, and incomplete and exposed electrical work which would have made any representative of the Health and Safety Executive turn a whiter shade of pale!

During my first tour of duty from 1959-61, I had been a member of Madras Gymkhana Club (MGC) and before I returned to England, perhaps it was a case of wishful thinking that for some reason or another I might return later, although at that time it did seem rather unlikely, or perhaps there was something of the prophetic about it, I don't know, but whatever the reason, I decided not to resign but instead to take out country membership. It proved a blessing in disguise, in that it only cost a relatively small amount to pay off membership arrears compared with having to pay quite a hefty amount as a new member; always providing that I had been accepted, which I feel was very unlikely in that the committee and membership was by then virtually all Indian! As such it had changed a great deal, but we were prepared and willing to be in a very small minority and after all it did provide us with the facilities we needed and I doubt if we could have claimed any grounds of racial discrimination! Because we were only out there for a relatively short time we were kept very busy and as a result we were fortunate that the factory at Ennore, where I worked previously, did supply us with a car for use during the times we were able to escape from the factory to the M.G.C. or the beach, or to Church on Sunday evening, usually St.Mary's in the Fort Saint George, where we were always made welcome, but because of the unpredictability of the work situation, it was not possible for me to take up any official duties.

One dark night I left my 'cell' and was out in the poorly lit compound on my way to the central building that housed the dining room, to look for something to read at bedtime when suddenly I saw stars, and I don't mean the heavenly variety; for in trying to avoid what I thought to be a pile of earth I had fallen into a deep storm drain, hitting my left chest on the edge of it. Fortunately it was not monsoon time, so it was empty, but I still do not know to this day how I managed to get out and find my way back to my 'bed-sit' and to summon the help of my colleague. The following morning, after a relatively sleepless night, I went in to work but was in a lot of pain, and because we were under 'military rule' I was sent to the military hospital at St Thomas's Mount, near to Meenambakkam Airport where I was examined and x-rayed and, because nothing was broken I was given the following treatment, 24 hrs bed rest, with hot water bottle and two paracetamol tablets! (somewhere in the archives I have the documentation to prove it) I certainly needed the bed rest, but when I noted from the bed list that 95% of the existing patients were suffering from venereal disease I decided that my 'cell' wasn't a bad place after all, and gladly returned to it!

Several days afterwards, because there was no improvement, I requested that I be seen by the works doctor from Ennore, Dr Ernest Somersakher, or stomach-shaker as he was affectionately known by the Leyland Technicians, and this was granted. He was a lovely man, an Anglo-Indian, and a Christian, and I will always remember the words of a Christmas card he sent me during my time at Ennore,

> Lord, as the shepherds came to Thee,
> With toil worn hands, all hastily:
> So we, from busy life would steal one hour,
> And at Thy cradle kneel.
> Pour on our wounds Thy healing balm,
> Give to our hearts Thine innermost calm:
> And, before we seek the world of men,
> Lord, take us to Thyself again

I had every confidence in Ernest, who, when he saw me, was anxious because of the delay and because he suspected internal bleeding. He sent me for further X-rays because he was of the opinion that although all the bruising was at the bottom of the rib cage, the real damage was elsewhere. He was right, the rib cage had in fact twisted in the fall and the break was in the second rib down on the left. Although I did not relish the idea, at least there was a reason for the pain, and with the right treatment I was soon on the mend, and it was good to meet my old friend again anyway! Which rather brings me back to the point of my telling you about my second visit to India, in that, like St.Paul on so many occassions, I have gone so far in my story and then gone off at a tangent before returning to the main theme, although there is a link, in that I now take up the story again with my reunion with one of the two Anglo-Indian gentlemen I talked about earlier, namely Mr.French, (Barnabas) the Verger at St.George's Cathedral in Madras.

It was a lovely sunny day, and the brightness of it was more than matched by the smile which greeted me as it had done so often before and his words of greeting so softy spoken but full of love and sincerity, "Mr Hunt, how lovely to see you again, I hope you are well, how are your wife and family? I hope you have time to stay and talk for a while so that I can bring you up to date". I reciprocated his greeting and assured him that I had time to stay and talk. Although, having said that, I spent most of the time we had together listening to all his news; how times had changed, the present staff members and how they compared with those in my day, and how much he preferred working with the new Bishop, rather than with Bishop Chellapa who by now had died, having always made clear, if not by word, certainly by attitude, his intense dislike of Anglo-Indians; so much so that it always surprised me not only how Mr.French managed to be appointed in the first place, but also how he managed to keep his job so long. No doubt it was because he was so good at it and because the Bishop had nothing to do with the hiring and firing. We also talked about our respective families and how we saw the possible future for us all. This being done I asked where Bishop Chellappa had been laid to rest, in that, so far as I was aware the Cathedral had no burial ground. "Come, and I will take you to his grave," he replied and took me out of the Cathedral and round the east end, where, immediately behind the High Altar, the grave was there for all to see, covered by a massive thick stone slab. I looked at Mr.French who had a faint smile on his face, and as he turned to me I said, "You have certainly made sure that he doesn't get out again very easily, haven't you!" He nodded his head and the faint smile was replaced with one much broader! How sad that a man who had so many qualities as a Father in God to his flock, should have been so unfeeling and insensitive to some of those in his care as a tarnish on his work and ministry, and on his memory as well. But from Mr French there was no resentment, he didn't harbour any grudges, yes, he had laughed at my comment, but inside there was a real sadness for all that had happened, "it could have been so much different, but it wasn't and all we can do is to forgive and to commend him to the love and mercy of Almighty God." We said our goodbyes, and as I walked away, I was aware that I had been with a very special man, who had given me hope and a great deal of food for thought!

During the time I was involved with our Spanish Associates E.N.A.S.A, I had the opportunity to visit their factories in Madrid and Barcelona and it was whilst in the former that I was able to visit Toledo; a very impressive Moorish city high on cliffs overlooking the meandering river far below, and housing not only the beautiful Cathedral dedicated to St.Mary the Virgin, but also the house of El Greco, (Domēnikos Theotokōpoulos) the renowned artist, a native of Crete, who spent much of his life in Toledo and died there in April 1614 at the age of 73. Toledo is also renowned for the finest sword steel and the most elaborate swords in the world, and there will be many homes like ours that have miniature swords made of Toledo steel as letter openers without realising it.

The Cathedral is magnificent and a veritable dream; it contains examples of every style of European architecture and of wood and stone carving through the centuries, whilst the crypt contains an abundance of treasures in silver, gold and precious stones. Behind the High Altar stands an enormous reredos of wood depicting various scenes from the life of Jesus, with the events of Holy Week, Easter day and the Ascension taking up at least one third of the

whole. One of the fascinating things about this lovely work of art, which is a
real masterpiece, is that apart from Jesus, all the rest of the characters, which
are almost life-size, are dressed in Spanish costume; which at first seems rather
strange, but then brings home the forcible reminder that this is exactly what
would still have happened if Toledo, and not Jerusalem, had been the scene
for all that happened long ago, and for me it brought a new meaning to the
words of the well-known spiritual, "Were you there when they crucified my
Lord?"

Further back, behind the reredos, but positioned on each side of it stand
the tombs of the Cardinals of Toledo, each in their own separate cell, each
quite ornate with the odd candle burning, though not at every one. There is
a tradition that when a cardinal dies, his hat is suspended from the ceiling by
a slender cord and when the cord breaks and the hat falls, it is a sign that the
soul of its owner has passed from purgatory into heaven. One or two have
already fallen, but others will have a while to wait yet, in that their hats are
held up, not by slender cords, but by a selection of chains! A gentle reminder
that even for the Princes of the Church there is a day of reckoning, not least
from those they have left behind! But in the centre of the tombs, immediately
behind the reredos and the High Altar it is a different story, for there, in
the place of honour, a flat and unadorned gravestone with the inscription in
Spanish which reads,

HERE LIES

DUST

ASHES

AND

NOBODY

No, it isn't the grave of an unknown soldier; it is the grave of the Prince
of Toledo at whose instigation, and by whose love and benevolence, the
Cathedral was built in the first place to the glory of God and dedicated to the
Blessed Virgin Mary.

Such love for God and for his people has made his grave the focal point for pilgrimage and prayer throughout the centuries since, and at the head of the grave are row upon row of lighted candles signifying the prayers and thanksgivings of the ordinary folk, standing out in sharp contrast to the tombs of the former Princes of the Church in comparative darkness nearby. Here the words of the Prophet Micah ring so true, "He, has showed you, O man, what is good. And what does the Lord require of you? To act justly and to love mercy and to walk humbly with your God." (Chapter 6 verse 8)

Whether this particular Prince of Toledo thought of himself in this way we will never know, but of one thing we can be sure and that is, that like the Princes of the Church and like Bishop Chellappa, he has left behind him both memories and a reputation that men respond to in one way or another, either kindly or unkindly as the case may be; but more important still, he has done so before the One to Whom all hearts are open, all desires known and from Whom no secrets are hidden; and at the end of the day it is His response that really matters!

It was this truth that came home to me quite forcibly in 2004, when I attended the funeral of a lovely man, William (Billy) Preston, who, in my early years at Leyland Motors taught me, and many more, in the Day Continuation School. A very sincere man with no airs and graces, but with a natural aptitude to teach, and to teach in a way that was not only easily understood but also retained without too much effort. A man, small in stature, but standing head and shoulders above the rest in the eyes of those of us privileged to sit at his feet; which is why there were so many of us present to say our farewells to him. Many of the faces I still knew well, although some I did not as is only natural considering the 'ravages' of the past fifty to sixty years, and come to think of it I wonder how many readily recognised me! But be that as it may, we could not but wonder how so much time had passed us by, and how quickly it had done so; what had we done with it, what story had we been writing, what memories and what reputation had we been building up day by day for future reference we knew not when? Yes, along with the many memories we shared together that day came a great deal of food for thought, and for me a deep sense of the urgent need to get my own priorities in order in the Spiritual sense of the word, and also to look again as a member of the Body of Christ, the Church, at those things with which the Church as a whole has had to contend during my membership of it; for in so many ways the world at large has made its feelings known in seeing the Church as irrelevant, out of touch, and seemingly unable or unwilling to deal with the problems of the twenty-first century in such a way as to give the world, leadership, hope and purpose. So that for those looking for an excuse not to be bothered or to opt out, the situation is ready made and many have voted with their feet already as the various surveys carried out on Church membership each year make abundantly clear; so much so, that instead of pussy-footing around, as has been the case for many years, there is a desperate need for a new vision in the field of evangelism, and also I believe, a still more desperate need for that self-examination and self-discipline which will lead to that spiritual cleansing without which the Church cannot be Christ-like or hope to lift Him up to the world in such a way as to enable Him to draw men to Himself; the very reason for its existence.

In the Western mainstream churches there has not only been a substantial fall-off in church attendance, but also in vocations as well. The Roman Catholic Church has suffered a sharp decline in respect of the latter, and the situation has been further exacerbated, if a television programme in 2003 is to be believed, by the resignation of many thousands of Priests and Nuns in renunciation of the Vow of Chastity (Celibacy) since 1960. Just how 'the powers that be' will ultimately deal with what has become a critical problem for them has yet to be seen; for although it is allowed for married men to serve as Deacons, any suggestion of this being extended further to include the Priesthood has not been taken up. To this end one wonders what advice St Peter, himself a married man, (St.Mark's Gospel chapter 1 verses 29-31) would have to offer his worthy Successor today. The Anglican Church has also experienced a fall off in vocations in the past few years, but the Ordination of Women, which eventually led to their being ordained to the Priesthood has done much to redress the situation, even taking into account the subsequent resignation of male clergy as a consequence of it; numbering in the Church of England alone between four and five hundred.

There has also been a serious undermining of the Church's teaching, reputation, credibility and respectability, by the involvement of clergy, male and female, in the sexual abuse of children and young people, often going back over long periods, in many cases with questions to be asked of those in high office who, in some instances were aware of the situation and did little or nothing about it. Even though the number of clergy involved amounts to only a small percentage of the whole work-force, nevertheless 'muck sticks,' as we would say up North, and the ongoing sideward glances and suspicion toward the rest of us can be very painful and counter productive from the pastoral point of view, in the building up of mutual trust and respect from an early age; and unless, and until, the Church as a whole makes it clear to the world that it will not tolerate such behaviour from those in Holy Orders, and takes the necessary action to discipline the perpetrators, nothing is going to change; and whilst no doubt the do-gooders will be quick to point out the need for love and understanding for those who have fallen by the wayside: they should read what the King of Love had to say on the matter, " whoso shall offend one of these little ones which believe in me, it were better for him that a millstone were hanged about his neck, and that he were drowned in the depth of the sea" (St Matthew chapter 18 verse 6 in King James Version). They may then appreciate that such discipline is a necessary factor not only from the point of view of the Church being seen to practice what it preaches and to show genuine concern for those who have been offended, but also as a first step towards possible restoration for the offenders should they wish to avail themselves of it.

It is at this point that we need to go back to basics, and to see the distinction between the Sacred and the secular, a distinction which in our modern high speed and materialistically minded world has been all but lost; such that everything is geared to the here and now and the effects of people's actions are judged by earthly standards and where little or no thought is given to the long term outcome; so much so that self, selfishness and greed, and the culture of "everyone doing what seems right in their own eyes" is now with us to an extent as perhaps never before experienced, with the consequences of it evident every day in our news bulletins. It is a culture that now affects every level of society, such that it will need far more than acts of Parliament to sort out, indeed, it will take nothing less than divine intervention. I don't mean the Second Coming of Jesus, although there is every indication that Biblically speaking we are now living in the last days; no I mean divine intervention in the sense of the Church once again being willing to stand up and be counted, in pointing out to a world at present more ready and willing to listen and respond to the temptations of the flesh and the devil, that in so doing it is on the path to self-destruction and completely at odds with the Sacred will and purposes of Almighty God for His world and for everyone and everything in it; and that it is only when the world is prepared to accept the Sacred over the secular that there can be any real hope for it now and for the future. But before it can do this, the Church, because it too has not escaped untouched by secularism, must, as I said earlier, be ready and prepared to undergo spiritual cleansing itself, regardless of the cost; in reflecting the spirit of the Psalmist when he writes, "Make me a clean heart O God: and renew a right spirit within me." (Psalm 51, verse 10. Book of Common Prayer)

This process will not be straight forward, because in the eyes of the world, much of what is a real problem within the Church is acceptable to the world at large as part of life as it perceives it to be at this moment of time, not least in matters of human sexuality. So far as society is concerned whatever happens between consenting adults behind closed doors is acceptable; and because God has given to every one of us the gift of freewill, the Church, to some extent, has to respect this view, although it is well aware that so far as God is concerned there are no closed doors and that much of what does happen in such circumstances may be outside the parameters of His will. So that whilst on the one hand those who wish to take advantage of the law in this respect as part of their 'human rights' should not deem it wrong or unfair for the Church to challenge their 'right' to the blessing of same sex relationships, or even to same sex marriages in the case of long term and exclusive partnerships, whilst at the same time acknowledging that it does have the duty of spiritual and pastoral care for those concerned. The problem is further compounded by the fact that because this matter involves the Sacred and the secular, there is little if any respect for the former by the latter, and therefore no consideration given to the on going effects which would follow the granting of such requests. Moreover there is also the added complication of those like-minded clergy who would be all too willing to perform such ceremonies given the opportunity! All of which means that the Church also has a dilemma with its openly Gay and Lesbian clergy which again needs to be considered sensitively and lovingly, and requires us once again to go back to basics.

When some Pharisees came to Jesus to test Him on the question of the lawfulness of a man divorcing his wife, His response is clear and to the point in that it first of all directs their thoughts to the Sacred Scriptures and then back in time to the creation of mankind, "Haven't you read," he replied, "that at the beginning the Creator 'made them male and female', and said, 'For this reason a man will leave his father and mother and be united to his wife, and the two will become one flesh'? So they are no longer two, but one. Therefore what God has joined together, let man not separate" (St.Matthew chapter 19, verses 4-6). In other words, what we are seeing here is not only the foundation principle for Christian marriage, but also a definition of heterosexual marriage as the norm according to the will and purpose of Almighty God for the on-going work of Creation; and, as such, by very definition, renders any act of homosexual intercourse, a sexual deviation that in no way can be seen as being equal to the norm in terms of its acceptability to the Creator, or ranking alongside the norm as regards requests for its acknowledgement by the Church on equal terms with the norm. All of which highlights the difference between the Sacred and the secular in that so far as the latter is concerned appeals can be made on the grounds of human rights, whereas in the case of the former the will of Almighty God can hardly be questioned, particularly on so fundamental an issue which is rooted and grounded in Holy Scripture. There are those, however, who would not agree with this, on the grounds that we are as God made us and that people should not be discriminated against because of their sexual makeup or orientation, either by the Church or anyone else, because we cannot help being what we are by nature. But to follow this argument through would lead to a virtually impossible situation, in that we would have to lay the blame for every single disfigurement deformity and imperfection at birth fairly and squarely at the door of God, regardless of any other factors such as parental generic and hereditary weaknesses that can so much influence the situation. And what about the effects of the drug Thalidomide, taken in good faith by so many expectant mothers during the early stages of pregnancy to prevent morning sickness, but with such disastrous consequences, or the consequences of a mother smoking or taking drugs during her pregnancy for her unborn child; are these also to be laid at God's door as well? The last few years have highlighted the wonder and delicate balance of human genes that are so much a part of our make up, and the influence they undoubtedly have on our nature in making us what we are. It is a very fine balance and consequently it has to be said that the argument that 'we are as God made us' and that, as a result, in the field of human sexuality our behaviour is not a deviation from the norm and therefore should be perfectly acceptable to the Sacred as well as the secular is, in my view and that of many others extremely tenuous, even to the point of being unsustainable, and particularly so in the case of those who are sexually active and who, having made the above claim, then proceed to become what they are not. This is not to say that their claims are to be dismissed out of hand, no, they are to be dealt with lovingly and with understanding because in the end the Church does have a pastoral responsibility for all concerned, even though they in turn may, in some instances, claim no allegiance to it. It would seem to me that the root of the problem lies not with a person's sexual orientation from birth, but whether that orientation leads to deviant sexual practice; and here we have a parallel case to that which Jesus refers to in the matter of marriage and divorce in Matthew chapter 19; for when the disciples said to Him, " If this is the situation between a husband and wife, it is better not to marry." Jesus replied, " Not everyone can accept this word, but only those to whom it has been given. For some are eunuchs (see below at *) because they were born that way; others, were made that way by men; and others have renounced marriage because of the kingdom of heaven. The one who can accept this should accept it." (Verses 10 and 11) In other words a person may be homosexual by orientation from birth, or through the influence of others, but this does not necessarily mean that this should result in sexual activity; it is a matter of choice in the application of our freewill, and it too, like marriage, can be renounced in celibacy to the glory of God. No one in his right mind would ever pretend that this is an easy option when it is generally recognised that the sexual urge is one of the strongest, if not the strongest urge in mankind, but it is possible, and many men and women have chosen that way.

There are many who would say that, compared with the host of other problems in the world today, the matter of human sexuality ranks low on the list and, in the secular sense, one would have to agree. But that is not the issue. The issue is that if the Church is to speak out and act with authority on the many problems in the world, it must, as far as is possible, be beyond reproach in terms of its own behaviour; and whilst it is easy to point the finger at the many times when, in the past, it has fallen from grace, many believe the time has come to do something about it. Which is why the Church has to deal with this matter in a positive way, for example, in asking whether clergy of either sex who are sexually active in same sex relationships, can be allowed to remain in office. Notice that I say, in office, not within the Church; because I am the first to recognise that they are, in the main, lovely, caring people, with so much to offer; but in a world which has gone 'sex mad' in so many ways, with pornography readily available and so often falling into young hands; with many programmes and even advertisements on television which are sexually motivated, together with the rise in this country in teenage pregnancies and an alarming increase in the instances of sexually transmitted diseases amongst teenagers are urgent causes for real concern: the Church's attitude is under close scrutiny and the need to put its own house in order is increasing by the hour. Nor, it has to be said, has the Church's cause been in any way helped by the recent Consecration of Canon Gene Robinson as Bishop of New Hampshire in the United States of America. Those who gave the Bishop his Christian name could never have envisaged how fitting it was for a man whose 'genes' meant that the picture of the moment of his Consecration could show, in the background, his two principal guests, namely his daughter from his heterosexual marriage and his present homosexual partner of 16 years; which I feel just about sums up what I have been endeavouring to say on this matter so far, and I feel sure that the Anglican Church will live to regret that it did not take the necessary action to prevent this happening. I also believe it still needs to act in the case of the Bishop as it does with other clergy in similar circumstances. In the meantime the Bishop shows no real signs of regret or remorse for what has sparked a crisis in Anglicanism, and in an article in the Church Times of 12th March 2004 he is reported as warning that the situation "would be messy for a while". This came from an interview the previous week for US CBS News network, in which he said that, even if he had stepped down, other "qualified, faithful, gay and lesbian folks" would come forward. "It's not all going to be back to being nice and pretty again." The article then goes on to report how, in responding to critics who say that it is a sin to be openly homosexual, the Bishop said: "In the eyes of some in my Church, it's a sin. And in the eyes of others in my Church, it's not. One of the great things about the Anglican tradition and the Episcopal Church in particular is that we have always disagreed about various and sundry issues, and yet come together around the altar rail." Having read his words I wonder at the acumen of the man! Surely the point at issue is not what one section or another of his Church thinks about the sin or otherwise of the openly homosexual, but what God thinks; and again, how can he, or indeed any of those clergy who participated in his consecration, claim allegiance to the Anglican Communion, in the knowledge that what they were doing does not have the support of the great majority of the members of that Communion and also that their own action would, and indeed has been, the cause of a crisis in Anglicanism and has put a great question mark against the willingness " to come together around the altar rail", in what could never be thought of in terms of "various and sundry" issues. The article closed with a reference to comments made by the Presiding Bishop at Canon Robinson's Consecration, the Most Revd Frank Griswold, in an interview for the Guardian newspaper where he said, "Certainly none of us had anticipated the effect of the Ordination (Consecration) in New Hampshire. It was telecast round the world. Possibly naïvely, we thought it was a local event." The article concluded with the Archbishop's comment that, "In the interests of the Anglican Communion" he had chosen not to respond to strong rhetoric from parts of the Anglican Communion.

In the opinion of many, the whole affair has been naïve in the extreme, and that it would be best remedied by the voluntary or enforced resignation of all concerned, preferably the former, in the interests of the Anglican Communion and of the whole Church of God.

In conclusion, one cannot deal with sensitive matters such as these without being very much aware of the need for soul searching in every area of the whole of the Church's membership; it is for each and every one of us to be honest to God and to ourselves about the many deviations from the norm of Christian life that have been part of our lives, and, if we are honest, the many times we too have fallen short of what God would have us be and do for Him. All of which should not only give us a real empathy with others in their need, but also a real determination to do all we can to sort out that little part of the Church that is us!

* In the Holman Bible Dictionary, we find the following definition of 'Eunuch' offered by M.Stephen Davis. "A male deprived of the testes or external genitals. Such were excluded from serving as priests (Leviticus, Chapter 21, verse 20) and from membership in the congregation of Israel (Deuteronomy, Chapter 23, verse 1). Eunuchs were regarded as especially trustworthy in the Ancient Near East and thus were frequently employed in royal service.

By extension, the Hebrew word translated eunuch could be used of any court official (at Genesis Chapter 37 verse 36 and Chapter 39, verse 1 the reference is to a married man). The Greek term translated eunuch is literally one in charge of a bed, a reference to the practice of using eunuchs as keepers of harems (Esther, Chapter 2, verses 3,6, and 15). Part of Isaiah's vision of the messianic era (when the Messiah came) was a picture of the eunuch no longer complaining of being 'a dry tree,' one without hope of descendants, because God would reward the faithful eunuch with a lasting monument and name in the Temple which would be far better than sons or daughters (Isaiah Chapter 56, verses 4-5). The Ethiopian eunuch of Acts, Chapter 8 verse 27 was reading from Isaiah's scroll. A 'eunuch for the sake of the kingdom of heaven' (Matthew chapter 19 verse 12) is likely a metaphor for one choosing single life in order to be more useful in kingdom work. Compare with 1 Corinthians chapter 7, verses 32-34."

Another matter of concern for many during my time in the Sacred Ministry, has been the Ordination of Women and in particular their Ordination to the Priesthood, which began with the service in Bristol Cathedral on March 12th 1994 when 32 Deacons were ordained Priest, of whom one has since died and fourteen have subsequently retired. An article in Church Times of 12 March 2004, observes that, "although women priests now make up a fifth of the total number of clergy in the Church of England, comparatively few are yet in senior appointments. The latest figures show 1262 full-time stipendiary women priests in dioceses, 715 non-stipendiary ministers (NSM), 208 ordained local ministers (OLM), and 212 chaplains. There are 72 women priests working in the Church Army, one Dean (although a second has been appointed), and five Archdeacons." The article was under the heading of 'Our journey isn't over, say women priests' and quotes a representative of the Bristol diocese, although it does not say whether clerical or lay, as saying that the journey would not be complete until women were made bishops and added "I'm not sure that waiting any longer will help people who find it a difficult idea." Although it would be hotly disputed by M.O.W (the Movement for the Ordination of Women), such a statement could be said to underline the feeling of many that the original intentions of the founders of the movement were motivated more by the secular than by the Sacred; that it was a movement by feminists to storm the one remaining bastion hitherto closed to them, the Priesthood, with every step towards success being greeted by not a little triumphalism. After all why not? We have a Queen of the realm and Titular Head of the Church of England; we have had a female Prime Minister; why not in time a female Archbishop of Canterbury? Women have the management skills; they have the necessary academic qualifications; so what is the problem, for on the face of it there would appear to be no reason why they cannot claim equality and equal opportunities with their male counterparts and get on with the matter. So why all the trouble which has led the Church of England to a crisis point, and has resulted in mass resignations of male priests on grounds of conscience numbering at the time of writing 430, with another 67 returning after resigning; as a serious loss, not only in terms of manpower but also as an untimely drain on finances under the Ordination of Women (Financial Provisions) Measure estimated to be in the region of £ 26,000,000? In fact there are those who would seriously question the need to pay out compensation at all, in that the introduction of the Ordination of Women to the Priesthood did not involve a change in the job description of those who chose to resign, albeit on the clause of conscience, it is therefore no longer grounds for compensation, as would certainly be the case in secular industrial practice. Furthermore, in the business world, any management who then chose to pay out compensation on such a scale would be deemed irresponsible, and could risk prosecution. Apart from this, it could also be argued that any employer who chose to introduce new legislation it knew could lead to such losses of manpower and funds in this day and age, would be held to be very dubious indeed, and especially so when it is so dependant on public support!

Such is the thinking on this matter if it is dealt with purely and simply in terms of the secular rather then the Sacred; and whilst it is not the purpose of this exercise to judge the management in question, even so I do feel it necessary for general information and consumption to air the points I have, in order that the reader might be able to make a balanced assessment and judgement of his or her own; and that said, like Paul I return to the main theme; that of endeavouring, in so far as we are able, to carry out a survey of the evidence in Holy Scripture as a whole in support or otherwise of the Ordination of Women to the Priesthood, so that we will then have not only a more complete picture of the whole evidence on which to base our individual opinions, but also the means to assess the thoughts of those who would say that to question the original motives of the founders of M.O.W. is wrong and would be in denial of God's will for the Church, the Body of His Son in the world.

First of all then to the Old Testament where woman is shown in at least two lights. The predominant view is one of woman in subjection to man, but at times woman is also the object of adoration and admiration. The creation stories in Genesis foreshadow two different perspectives regarding woman. In the account in Genesis Chapter 1,verses 26-30, man and woman are created simultaneously: woman, like man, is made in the image of God, and together man and woman reflect that image and woman therefore is not in an inferior place to man in creation. In Genesis Chapter 2, verses 7-25, (Chapter 2 is thought to come from an earlier source than Chapter 1) it is a different story. Here man is created before woman and woman is viewed as being created from man, for man, as his helper. This account is also cited in support of the view that woman should remain subject to man since she has a subordinate position in creation, although in verse 18 she is spoken of as a 'suitable partner/helper'. In the story of the Fall of Man in Genesis Chapter 3, it is Eve who is portrayed as the first to fall to the temptation of the serpent, and as the agent for the temptation of Adam, and consequently she is told by God, "I will greatly increase your pain in childbearing; with pain you will give birth to children. Your desire will be for your husband, and he will rule over you."

The subordination of woman also appears more clearly in the Ten Commandments, firstly, in their being addressed to men, evidenced by the use of masculine pronouns, and secondly, in the final commandment where there is reference to man not coveting any of his neighbour's property, his neighbour's wife is included in the list of possessions (Exodus, chapter 20, verse 17).

Marriage and divorce are also areas in which woman's rights were subordinate to those of man. For example, if a woman about to be married was suspected of not being a virgin, she was required to submit to a test, and if her virginity was not established, she could be stoned to death at her father's door, (Deuteronomy Chapter 22, verses 13-21) whereas no such requirement was made of a man. Adultery also, was seen as a crime against a husband's rights, and whilst both the male and female caught in the act of adultery were stoned, it was to vindicate the husbands rights. (Verse 22) A man who had fears about his wife's faithfulness could take her to the priest for further examination to determine her guilt or otherwise, but no such avenue was available to the woman.

Divorce was also biased toward the husband. He could obtain a divorce from his wife "because he finds something indecent about her" (Deuteronomy Chapter 24 verse 1), the words "indecent" or "objectionable" being variously interpreted as anything from adultery to burning the toast!

In so far as religious law was concerned, inequality between boy and girl babies existed from the very beginning of life. A mother who bore a baby girl was considered unclean for twice as long as a mother who bore a male child. During her "purifying" time after the birth, a mother "was not to touch any holy thing, or enter the sanctuary until the days of her purification are over, for during that time the woman will be unclean, as during her period and must wait the required time to be purified from her bleeding"(Leviticus, Chapter 12 verses 2-5).

Against what appears to be a predominance of woman in subordinate roles, there are several more positive images in the Old Testament. Undoubtedly, woman was venerated in her role as wife and mother and in the Ten Commandments one's duty is to honour both father and mother (Exodus Chapter 20 verse 12), whilst in the Book of Proverbs Chapter 31 verses 10-

end, the ideal woman is seen as a wife and mother, who, besides fulfilling both roles also engages profitably in the business world as well.

The birth of children is also seen as a sign of God's favour bestowed upon a good woman, and particularly so in the birth of male children (Genesis chapter 29 verse 31 to chapter 30 verse 24).

The story of Ruth is a very good example of a traditional woman who was admired for her role as a good daughter-in-law. She, and her Mother-in-law Naomi, whose husbands had both died, were women of worth whom God aided by sending Boaz as their protector. In time, he and Ruth were married and eventually became the great-grandparents of King David (Book of Ruth chapters 1-4): nor would any summary of the Old Testament evidence be complete without reference to the treatment of women in a still more positive way as typified in Proverbs chapter 1 verse 20 where Wisdom, which held high value for the Hebrew people, is personified as "she". Then again, the prophet Isaiah uses a mother's love for her child as a model for God's love for His people (Isaiah chapter 49 verse 15 and chapter 66 verse 13), whilst several women, including Miriam, Deborah, Huldah and Esther all earned the respect and admiration of the Israelite nation by playing significant roles in times of national crisis.

We now turn from the Old Testament to the New, where, in general, we find that Jesus was able to retain the best in the Hebrew tradition and yet cut away some of the rigid structure that in so many ways restricted it. He was also able to do the same for woman. Without radically changing her roles, Jesus enlarged and transformed a woman's possibilities for a full life; His manner and teachings elevated her status and gave her an identity and a cause, whilst His manner in His exchanges with women is at least as significant as His teachings about woman. At the risk of censure from a male-orientated society, Jesus talked to women, responded to their touch, healed them, received their emotional and financial support, and used them as main characters in His stories. Jesus saw them, not as possessions, but as persons; and when Martha, the sister of Mary and Lazarus, wanted Jesus to make her sister help with the serving duties, He affirmed Mary's choice to learn as a disciple. Women of that day could not be disciples of rabbis, but Jesus recognised women's potential for intelligent thought and commitment (St Luke, chapter 10 verses 38-42).

On another occasion, Jesus welcomed a woman's anointing of His head as an indication of her understanding of His real mission, and instead of rejecting her public display or chiding her for her extravagance, He commended her for her act of love for which he said she would be remembered wherever the Gospel was preached throughout the world, and in so doing Jesus treated her as a person of insight and feeling (St Mark chapter 14 verses 3-9). His meeting with the woman at the well in Samaria is yet another example of Jesus seeing women as persons, such that He was not restricted in His conversation with her, either by her sex or by her race (St John chapter 4 verses 1-26). Again, Jesus treated the woman taken in adultery in the same way, as a person. He did not condone her action, but neither did he allow her to be subjected to a double standard by her male accusers. Instead, He offered her a new start with new possibilities and His personal directive: "Neither do I condemn you, go now and leave your life of sin" (St John, chapter 8 verses 1-11).

Not only did Jesus see and treat women as persons in their own right, He also welcomed them and involved them in His earthly ministry. In St Luke, chapter 8 verses 1-3, we read "After this, Jesus travelled about from one town and village to another, proclaiming the good news of the kingdom of God. The twelve were with him, and also some women who had been cured of evil spirits and diseases: Mary (called Magdalene) from whom seven demons had come out; Joanna the wife of Chuza, the manager of Herod's household, Susanna and many others. These women were helping to support them out of their own means." Women also proclaimed the Gospel, for example the Samaritan woman at the well, mentioned above, who, having heard Jesus reveal Himself as the Messiah, immediately left and began telling people, and in St John, chapter 4 verse 39, we have evidence of her words and their success "Many of the Samaritans from that town (Sychar) believed in him because of the woman's testimony, 'He told me everything I ever did.'" Nor would Jesus have been unimpressed by the insight and intuition of the wife of Pontius Pilate, in the message she sent to him in his dilemma of dealing with the crowd baying for the blood of Jesus, "Don't have anything to do with that innocent man, for I have suffered a great deal today in a dream because of him" (St Matthew, chapter 27 verse 19).

Matthew, Mark and particularly Luke, all call attention to the loyalty of the women who participated in the Galilean ministry of Jesus and who followed Him all the way to the cross and the tomb; they were the first at the tomb on Easter Day and the first witnesses of the Resurrection; they were the first to hear the greatest news and to share it with others, "Why do you look for the living among the dead? He is not here; he has risen! Remember how he told you, while he was still with you in Galilee: 'The Son of Man must be delivered into the hands of sinful men, be crucified and on the third day be raised again.' Then they remembered his words and when they came back from the tomb they told all these things to the Eleven and to all the others." (St Luke, chapter 24, verses 5-9)

In His parables, Jesus reaches out to men and women in their own right, by telling stories from their life. "Suppose one of you has a hundred sheep and loses one of them. Does he not leave the ninety-nine in the open country and go after the lost sheep until he finds it? And when he finds it, he joyfully puts it on his shoulders and goes home" (St Luke, chapter 15 verses 4-7). "Or suppose a woman has ten silver coins and loses one. Does she not light a lamp, sweep the house and search carefully until she finds it?" (St Luke, chapter 15 verses 8-10). In the mind of Jesus, the woman searching for her lost coin represented God's activity in seeking for the lost, equally as much as the man searching for his lost sheep; just as in the same way, His parables of the man who planted a mustard seed (the smallest of all seeds) in his garden and it became a tree where the birds of the air perched in its branches, and the woman who took yeast and mixed it into a large amount of flour until it worked all through the dough (St Luke chapter 13 verses 18-21), meant the involvement of both in working for the kingdom of God.

Furthermore, Jesus also knew that marriage and divorce were both issues of great importance to women since their main roles were those of wife and mother; and as such He was very much aware as to how much their emotional, social and financial security was closely dependant on the strength or otherwise of their marriages. And although He knew what the Jewish Law had to say on these matters, He was not slow in making religion a matter of the heart instead of the rather mechanical observance of the multitude of minute details that had been laid down. He saw divorce as a testimony to the hardness of the human heart and not the will of God, and He told those who were casually divorcing their wives, often for the most petty and mundane of reasons, and then marrying again, that they were in fact committing adultery (St Matthew chapter 19 verses 1-9). Responsive to the plight of women, Jesus offset the male bias towards divorce and strengthened marriage as a permanent union. He saw women as neither inferior or superior, He saw their potential, their sinfulness, their strengths and weaknesses, and He dealt with them directly; and whilst as a group He elevated their status and strengthened and encouraged their participation and influence in the world, as individuals, He treated them as friends and disciples even though they did not number among the Twelve; nor must we forget the wonderful relationship Jesus enjoyed with Mary and Martha, the sisters of his dear friend Lazarus, and how he dealt with them and their problems, (St Luke chapter 10 verses 38-42 and St John chapter 11 verses 17-37).

But how were these views of Jesus reflected in the early Church, and particularly so, when for so long, the teachings of Jesus were passed on by word of mouth until they were written down in the Four Gospels? The answer is that we must turn to the Epistles or Letters of St Paul, all of which were written before the Gospel of Mark, which was the first of the Four Gospels to be written.

In his letter to the Galatians Paul deals with many problems there, (as indeed was the reason for most if not all his letters to other Churches and individuals as well) but also in addition, he gives to them and to his readers of every generation, his vision that with God there is no partiality among persons. Hence in chapter 3 verses 27-28 we read, "for all of you who were baptised into Christ have clothed yourselves with Christ. There is neither Jew nor Greek, slave nor free, male nor female, for you are all one in Christ Jesus." As I see it, what Paul is saying here is that "in Christ Jesus" we are one, but only in so far that we are submissive and obedient to His will and not our own. The potential is there as God's free gift and requires our free and unconditional acceptance!

In his Second Letter to the Corinthians, chapter 11verse 28, Paul writes, "Besides everything else, I face daily the pressure of my concern for all the churches"; a reminder to us all that pressure of work is nothing new for those who love and serve the Lord! Paul certainly felt the tension of maintaining order, and because of his background, his pedigree and credentials, which he details in his Letter to the Philippians, chapter 3, verses 4-6, he often falls back on the Jewish social customs of the day in order to ensure that the particular young church to whom he is writing is not seen in an unfavourable light. But having said that, he was also a man of his time with a vision, and was prepared to take risks. We see this in his Letter to the Ephesians, chapter 5 verses 21-33, where he moves ahead of his Jewish background in calling for mutual submission between husbands and wives, and in so doing Paul is reflecting the concern of Jesus that all relationships should reflect the grace extended by God, and the responsibilities of both husbands and wives to love each other follow the initial exhortation to "Submit to one another out of reverence for Christ", in verse 21; furthermore when Paul speaks of submission, it is not in a military sense , but rather as a loving sacrificial response.

Paul is also concerned that Christians should neither cause offence to others, nor be a stumbling-block to cause them to fall into sin; rather let everything be done to the glory of God. "So whether you eat or drink or whatever you do, do it all for the glory of God. Do not cause anyone to stumble, whether Jews, Greeks or the church of God - even as I try to please everybody in every way. For I am not seeking my own good but the good of many, so that they may be saved" (1 Corinthians chapter 10 verses 31-33); a thought also reflected in chapter 8 verse13 of the same letter.

Alongside Paul's words about women, we also need to see how these were reflected in his dealings with them; how did he relate to them in practice? In general he welcomed them as co-labourers in the churches and commended them for their gifts and faithfulness. "I commend to you our sister Phoebe, a servant of the church in Cenchrea. I ask you to receive her in the Lord in a way worthy of the saints and to give her any help she may need from you, for she has been a great help to many people, including me. Greet Priscilla and Acquila, my fellow workers in Christ Jesus. They risked their lives for me. Not only I but all the churches of the Gentiles are grateful to them" (Romans, chapter 16 verses 1-4). How women help in transmitting the faith is seen in 2 Timothy, chapter 1 verse 5; and when Paul speaks in 1 Corinthians chapter 12 about the gifts of the Holy Spirit poured out upon the Church, he evidently relies upon women to exercise their gifts as a part of the Body of Christ. But having said this, no resume of the evidence available to us in this respect would be complete without reference to Paul's thoughts and instructions regarding the position of women in worship, as detailed in his First Letter to Timothy, chapter 2 verses 8-15, "I want men everywhere to lift up holy hands in prayer, without anger or disputing. I also want women to dress modestly, with decency and propriety, not with braided hair or gold or pearls or expensive clothes, but with good deeds, appropriate for women who profess to worship God. A woman should learn in quietness and full submission. I do not permit a woman to teach or to have authority over a man; she must be silent. For Adam was formed first, then Eve. And Adam was not the one deceived; it was a woman who was deceived and became a sinner. But women will be saved through childbearing - if they continue in faith, love and holiness with propriety."

Whilst these final thoughts of Paul, may not fit in well with the thinking of the modern, emancipated and self-assured woman of the 21st century, they are nevertheless the words of Holy Scripture and therefore must be taken into consideration in the overall assessment of women's place and potential in the Church today and in particularly as regards their Ordination as Priests; and as Christians turn to the Bible for guidance in responding to this and other important issues, which affect not only individual churches but also their unity, they and we, must be careful not to focus on one verse or passage which promotes our particular cause one way or the other, but rather to concentrate prayerfully on the whole impact and message which the Bible as a whole is proclaiming. And in just the same way, it would not be right to judge this very important issue by focussing, without due regard for what the Holy Bible has to say, on 21st Century ideas of sexual equality and equal opportunities.

It would appear from the evidence we have considered here, that whilst it does without doubt support the role of women in the Church; a fact which is also underlined by the history of the Church; and they are urged to use their responsibility as well as their freedom to find their place in the Body of Christ, it is the feeling of many who have thought long, hard, and prayerfully about it, that the weight of evidence, whilst it does allow for their admission as Deacons, does not appear to be sufficiently in favour of their being ordained as Priests. This being said, the right for all of us to have our own opinions on this delicate matter has to be respected even if they lead to a different conclusion. I only wish it were an easier and more clear- cut matter to decide, but alas that is not the case and we must continue to think and pray about it.

In conclusion, the question of whether the belief of many that the original intentions of M.O.W. were motivated more by the secular than by the Sacred can be refuted, must therefore remain open, as the answer is known only to those involved, and because like faith it does not depend upon "feelings, fond and fugitive" but upon the will and word of God, it has to be said that, in the opinion of many, the jury is still out in spite of the General Synod's decision to proceed, and that ultimately, in mutual love and respect for each other 'in the Lord', it may be a case of 'letting both grow together until the harvest,' not in the original context of our Lord's Parable of the Wheat and the Tares, but as labourers together in the Lord's Vineyard.

The Feast of the Annunciation on 25th March 2004, with its lovely story of the announcement to Mary that she had been chosen by God to be the Mother of His Son, and how she responded in humble acceptance to this staggering news to a young teenager; was the day upon which we were invited, as clergy and congregation, to join our nearby Roman Catholic brethren to share with them in 'The Stations of the Cross' as part of our Lenten discipline and preparation for Easter. It marked yet another stage in the special relations our two congregations have enjoyed since the arrival of their present Parish Priest Fr. John Cribben and our own Vicar Canon Roy McCullough. I found the whole service meaningful, exciting and inspiring, in being able to walk, step by step, in readings and prayer, the Via Dolorosa (The way of the Cross); something that we had hoped to be able to do in a visit to the Holy land we had planned whilst on holiday in Cyprus, but which sadly had to be aborted due to the Gulf War. Attending this service in Our Lady and St.Patrick's Church also brought back many memories of my early years, when, quite frankly, to even attend a service there was unthinkable, out of bounds and very much frowned upon; as I discovered on the few occasions I was disobedient or was it rebellious, I don't know. The fact was that a lot of my young friends were Roman Catholics and I went along with them to see what happened that was thought to be so bad, and in the hope that I would not be found out! But inevitably the news leaked out and I had to suffer the consequences, unpleasant at the time but which I now see as being my earliest contributions towards Christian Unity, which in so many ways has been, and indeed still is, a painful, not to mention painfully slow procedure.

I found the service, The Way of the Cross - The Traditional Devotion newly presented by Andrew Moore - very moving, sensitive and reassuring, not least in the alternative prayer at the Third, Seventh, and Ninth Stations which tell how Jesus fell under the weight of His Cross; a prayer not only for our Lenten preparation, but also for every day of our lives.

> Lord Jesus,
> when we fall, as sure we will,
> have mercy on us;
> when we fall, as sure we will,
> give us strength and new hope;
> when we fall, as sure we will,
> forgive us and make us yours.
> For you are Lord, for ever and ever.
> Amen.

After the service Fr.John expressed what I feel sure were the thoughts of all the congregation, when he said how much, during the service, he had experienced and rejoiced in the feeling of togetherness, an atmosphere which he said was "so strong and so real, that you could almost cut it with a knife"; that feeling of togetherness, which is called Christian Unity, and which is the natural outcome when those who are gathered together in His Name, have their minds fixed on Jesus; when, in effect, they let go and let Him. It takes courage, it means taking risks, it means a ready willingness to stand up and be counted, it means for all concerned some loss for the sake of the One, Who in His love for us was prepared to do all of these things and to give His all.

This is not the place, nor is it the intention of the writer, to give a chronological account of the progress by the various Churches in Christendom towards visible unity; what we might call the 'official line', because in the main, it would only highlight yet again and again, the things, such as authority and the differences in teachings and disciplines, which separate us one from the other, rather than an earnest attempt to cherish and develop those things which we have in common, one Lord, one Faith, one Baptism, one God and Father of us all.

In a quiet moment for reflection halfway through the Way of the Cross, I looked up to the crucifix suspended high above the entrance to the sanctuary, giving silent, yet powerful testimony to those words of Isaac Watts in his lovely hymn 'when I survey the wondrous cross'; loved by so many and already referred to in the second chapter of this book,

See from His head, His hands, His feet,
Sorrow and love flow mingled down;
Did e'er such love and sorrow meet,
Or thorns compose so rich a crown?

Were the whole realm of nature mine,
That were an offering far too small,
Love so amazing, so divine,
Demands my soul, my life, my all.

Words so moving, and so challenging, not just for each of us individually as members of His Body the Church, but also for the Church as a whole, and particularly so as regards Christian Unity.

On the night before He died Jesus shared the Passover meal with His Disciples in the Upper Room, and in the Gospels of Matthew (Chapter 26 verses 17 - 35), Mark (Chapter 14 verses 12-31), and Luke (Chapter 22 verses 7-38), we are given quite a lot of detail as to what happened at 'The Last Supper', but apart from the words of Jesus over the Bread and Wine and His prediction of Peter's denial of Him, no other details of what Jesus had to say. It is John who, as it were, lifts the veil, and allows us to listen to the many things He had to say to His followers, and the prayers He said for Himself, His Disciples and for all believers (Chapter 13 verse 1 - Chapter 17 verse 26).

His third prayer for all believers, is for you and for me, and for all who have come to believe in Jesus through the message of those first Disciples of His; and the overriding plea in prayer of Jesus to His Father is that we should be One, as they are One, "My prayer is not for them alone (His Disciples there at the time). I pray also for those who will believe in me through their message, that all of them may be one, Father, just as you are in me and I am in you. May they also be in us so that the world may believe that you have sent me. I have given them the glory that you gave me, that they may be one as we are one: I in them and you in me. May they be brought to complete unity to let the world know that you sent me and have loved them even as you have loved me" (Chapter 17 verses 20-23).

When we pray to God, asking for help, strength, guidance, reassurance, or a particular blessing either for ourselves or someone in need; in general, we do so with the earnest expectation that God, in His good time, and in His own particular way, which will be for the best for all concerned, will do something about it as He sees best, but hopefully soon! Well, we know that God's time is not our time in matters eternal, but how must Jesus feel over 1970 years after His prayer in the Upper Room, to know that prayer has still not been answered? But His prayer to the Father was not for the Father to make us one, it was a loving expression of His deepest desire that our oneness should reflect the Oneness He shared with His Father, and anything more than that, which would have meant the imposition of Unity from 'on high' would have been a denial of God's gift of freewill. All of which means that the fact that Jesus' deepest desire is still unfulfilled, lies not at God's door, but at ours; and, what is more, despite the passage of so much time there appears to be no real sign of a solution to the problem either, particularly from the 'official' point of view, for apart from visits of leaders to each other and the setting up of consultative bodies, for example, A.R.C.I.C, between the Roman Catholic and Anglicans, and 'Conversations' between Anglicans and Methodists, very little else appears to have happened in my lifetime, except for the emergence of the Church of South India, inaugurated on the 27thof September 1947, and in which I was privileged to serve from 1959-1961. Any progress that has been made apart from this has been, not at official level but at grass-roots level, in ordinary folk realising their need for each other, the need to grow together, to understand and to share with each other the riches which are so much a part of all denominations; and all of this against a growing impatience with the hierarchies of those denominations dragging their feet, and in so doing, not only disregarding the deepest wish of Jesus that we should be one, but also in effect perpetuating the deep divisions which are an offence to His Name and must cause Him pain.

Why has all this been allowed to happen? What justification do the leaders of the Churches of Christendom have to offer? What valid reasons can they possibly offer for the present state of things to the one head of the Body of Christ, Jesus Himself, to support their behaviour before Him? What He left behind was a family and a family meal together with words of guidance and encouragement and a prayer for unity, consequently He gives no credence to individual denominations, which He sees as fragmentation of His family, and their claims to have this or that advantage over the rest are not only unacceptable to Him, but also a cause of concern and sadness to His heart. Maybe it is because, in addition to being an Anglican, I am also distantly related to the English Martyr St.John Southworth, that I feel the need for such courage to stand up and be counted today, come what may, in challenging all the leaders within the Church of God to recognise that the prayer of Jesus has gone unanswered for far too long and that it is high time that they do something about it now, before it is too late! At a time when much effort is being expended in inter-Faith dialogue, there is a more deeper need than ever to get our own priorities in order, "May they be brought to complete unity to let the world know that you have sent me and have loved them even as you have loved me"(St John chapter 17 verse 23).

The road to complete unity will not be an easy one, but it will be a joyful one when undertaken in love for the One Who has loved us so much, and no doubt the birth of the Church of South India has a lot to say to those who seek to walk it.

It involved the union of three religious bodies: the Anglican Church of India, Burma and Ceylon in respect of four of its dioceses, i.e Madras, Tinnevelly, Travancore with Cochin, and Dornakal; the South India Province of the Methodist Church; and the South India United Church, itself the result of a movement which brought together Presbyterians, Congregational and Dutch Reformed bodies. All in all quite a mixed bunch, and in many ways strange bed fellows, but all of whom were convinced of the need to step out in faith. In and through the power and guidance of the Holy Spirit, the new Church claimed to be a united and visible Church, in which the Congregational, Presbyterian, and Episcopal elements were preserved, and although at that time it was not wholly Episcopal, provisions were made that by the end of an interim period of say 30 years, all its presbyters would be episcopally ordained. In the meantime, there were no restrictions on inter-communion except Holy Baptism, and apart from that, the invitation to Holy Communion was 'to all who love the Lord'; in other words it was seen as the Sacrament of growing into complete unity, rather than as the ultimate symbol of complete unity, which seems to be the 'official' aim at this time; and because of which the Roman Catholic Church has laid down strict rules preventing its members from receiving Holy Communion elsewhere, much to the sadness of many. Perhaps we ought to remember that on their last night together before Jesus died it was the meal that came first and then the discourse and prayers afterwards; and it could be said that Jesus wanted it to go on in that way. The early Church certainly maintained the order as we read in Acts 2 verse 42, "They devoted themselves to the apostles' teaching and to the fellowship, to the breaking of the bread and to prayer." At the very heart of their growing together was the family meal Jesus had given them; it was from it that they gained strength, guidance and reassurance, it was necessary for their very being that they should be able to share it with each other, and in it to be one with their risen Lord!

So I hope you will agree that the Church of South India, still flourishing today, well over fifty years on, has a great deal to say to our leaders today, and although we may be frustrated by the thought that "like a mighty tortoise moves the Church of God", there is hope, and that hope will grow and bear fruit in abundance when we make the prayer of Jesus our own, in doing all we can to further it where we are, and in praying day by day for those in authority that they will drag their feet no more, but rather through the power and guidance of the Holy Spirit, become men and women of courage and vision; as those who by their faith in, and loyalty to, Jesus, are instrumental in bringing a long awaited and resounding Amen to His prayer that we may all be one as He and the Father are One!

Creator of rainbows,
come through the closed doors
of our emotions, mind and imagination;
come alongside us as we walk,
come to us at work and worship,
come to our meetings and councils,
come and call us by name,
call us to pilgrimage.

Wounded healer,
out of our dis-unity
may we be re-membered,
out of the pain of our division,
may we see your glory.
Call us from present
pre-occupation
to future community.

Spirit of Unity,
challenge our preconceptions,
enable us to grow in love and understanding,
accompany us on our journey together,
that we may go out with confidence
into your world as a new creation -
one body in you,
that the world may believe. Amen.

Kate McIlhagga. (From 'The Green Heart of the Snowdrop')

Loving Lord,
long ago you prayed that we should be one,
as you and the Father are One:
we confess that because of our selfishness, pride,
bigotry and unwillingness to let go of those things
which are the causes of our unhappy divisions, we still
persist in causing you pain, by failing to fulfil your deep
desire for us all;

fill the hearts and minds of all those in authority with a
new vision of your glory, a new sense of longing for your
will to be done on earth as it is in heaven, and a new spirit
of adventure, where your will for us is paramount, and all
the hostility, antagonism, distrust and misunderstandings of
past years can, and will, be laid aside in loving obedience to
your word, and in complete dependence on your power to heal
and to make all things new;

help us, as we wait upon you in eager expectation, to continue
steadfast, in prayer for each other and for your guidance and
protection, that we may serve you in one another, and love each
other as you love us;

for you are alive and reign with the Father and the Holy Spirit,
one God, now and forever. Amen.

Alan Hunt

THE EPILOGUE

Lord, for the years your love has kept and guided,
Urged and inspired us, cheered us on our way,
Sought us and saved us, pardoned and provided:
Lord of the years, we bring our thanks today.

Lord for that Word, the Word of life which fires us,
Speaks to our hearts and sets our souls ablaze,
Teaches and trains, rebukes us and inspires us:
Lord of the Word, receive your people's praise.

Lord for our land, in this our generation,
Spirits oppressed by pleasure, wealth and care:
For young and old, for commonwealth and nation,
Lord of our land, be pleased to hear our prayer.

Lord, for our world, where men disown and doubt you,
Loveless in strength, and comfortless in pain,
Hungry and helpless, lost indeed without you:
Lord of the world, we pray that Christ may reign

Lord for ourselves; in living power remake us -
Self on the cross and Christ upon the throne,
Past put behind us, for the future take us:
Lord of our lives, to live for Christ alone.

Timothy Dudley-Smith 1926-
(Hymn 428, Complete Mission Praise)

A t this stage in my thoughts, I see the penultimate line of the above
hymn in a new light, for in a very real sense in the foregoing I have
put the past behind me, even though very close to my heart and a real part of
my life it will always be, and have endeavoured to look forward to what lies
ahead. It is therefore, both a time for thanksgiving, as the above hymn so well
expresses, and also a time for consolidation and expectation of what the future
holds. Having been made very conscious, as I said in the Prologue, of my own

mortality and the need to put down in words things that have happened to me 'Through all the changing scenes of life' while I have the opportunity; I have done so with the earnest hope and prayer that they will encourage you and all who read them to take a good long hard look at all that has happened to you in your life, and to draw out from it the many and varied ways in which God in His love for us, draws near to us and through those experiences also draws us nearer to Himself.

In so many ways I feel blessed in having been given as it were a second chance, and so many people, 'bless em' have said, "obviously it wasn't time, there is still a lot more for you to do"; maybe it was to write this book, or to continue as Honorary Assistant Priest in the team at St.Leonard's Church, and as Honorary Chaplain to St.Catherine's Hospice, in addition to caring for my Wife; who knows, and for how long! Soon after my recovery from surgery and my return to 'active service', one of our parishioners, Elizabeth, a very sincere, prayerful, born-again Christian, came to me with a word of prophecy, she said, "Just like King Hezekiah you have been given another fifteen years!" (You will find the story in 2 Kings chapter 20 verses 1-7). The proof of prophecy is that it eventually comes to pass, and all that I can say at the time of writing is that there are now thirteen years to go and still counting; each day being greeted with thanksgiving and lived out to the very best of our ability as a daily walk with the Lord, confident in Him that He will, in His own good time and in His own loving way, bring it to completion and fulfilment.

When I was the Curate of Standish, the Rector, Rev. Canon. C.E. ('Peter') Bramley and I were invited to conduct a mission in Southport and nearby Churchtown; he as the main speaker, and I as his warm up man, 'getting them in the mood' through dialogue with them, and in practising the hymns suitable for the particular session; all in all a very interesting and enlightening experience for all concerned! The Rector's last talk was on the subject of 'Death and Beyond', in which he began by relating the reply of a clergy friend of his, who, having been asked what he was going to do in retirement said, "I am going to prepare, to the best of my ability, to meet the One I have been serving and preaching about for the past forty years!" I have never forgotten his words and the importance of what they are saying, not just for those in the Ordained Ministry but for us all; underlining as they do the importance and urgency of getting our priorities in order. I don't mean this in terms of getting our worldly affairs in order, in making our minds up what to do with our earthly possessions when we have no further use for them; in leaving the necessary instructions in order to avoid any 'misunderstandings' when the time comes and when 'relatives' come out of the woodwork to stake their claims! No, important as this may be, I mean something far deeper and more personal; I mean coming to terms with how we stand in our relationship or otherwise with God. In asking ourselves honestly and sincerely where we feel we really are in that relationship, if it exists at all; whether we are satisfied with it; or whether we feel the need to do something about it. Many in our world today have no time for God, or so they say, until something goes wrong in sickness, bereavement, or tragedy, and then the one for whom they have no time becomes their first port of call for help. Just as there are also many who see Jesus as an optional extra in life, as a good man and a teacher, who performed miracles of healing and feeding the multitudes, who set us an example of how to live and help other people which we can either accept and adopt for ourselves or not as we prefer. But whilst on the face of it, these things can be said to be true in themselves, there is no way in which Jesus can ever be thought of as an optional extra, for He lies at the very heart of God's plan for the world He has made, and so that in love we may share in His life both here and in eternity. Without Jesus, there is no hope beyond this life, and without Jesus, there is no real forgiveness or fulfilment in this life either. He is central to everything, and therefore if we feel content with life as it is and do not feel that we have need for anything or anyone further, not even Jesus, because we have lived a good life and done everything we can to help other people and have never done anyone any harm; in other words, if there is a heaven, we are quite capable of getting in there under our own steam and don't need any help thank you very much; then, although we may not feel we have any real problems to come at this moment in our lives, how confident are we that this will continue to be the case, and what will we have to say on that day when, as St. Paul writes in Romans, chapter 14 verses 10-12, "We will all stand before God's judgement seat"? "It is written: 'As surely as I live' says the Lord, 'Every knee will bow before me; every tongue will confess to God. So then, each of us will give an account of himself to God.'" Words to be dealt with, not only by those who at this stage of the proceedings are feeling able to cope with them under their own steam, but by all of us; which is why this book has at its heart, an appeal from the heart, to look again at your life, as I have endeavoured to look at mine, to rediscover for yourself the ways in which, through experiences and people, God has reached out to you, spoken to you and given you guidance in ways and at times, which, for one reason or another, have passed from your memory, but which will come flooding back, as they did for me, once you set out on the journey of rediscovery.

That journey has reminded me of the many wonderful people it has been my privilege to know, some of whom I have mentioned by name, but countless more who will always have a very special place in my heart and whose memory I will always treasure.

That journey has also taught me the vital importance and privilege of saying prayers, 'arrow' and otherwise, to Almighty God, at any second of day or night, knowing that He is always there and will answer them in a way that will be best for all concerned.

Throughout that journey through all the changing scenes of life, I have learned to take each step and to live each day with Jesus, who died for me, who is my Saviour and my friend who has shared with me in those times on that journey when all has seemed very dark, and has carried me when my own strength has failed me. It has also taught me what a precious and priceless privilege we have in Prayer and in sharing in the Blessed Sacrament of Holy Communion; to meet with and be fed by the One in and through Whom all things are possible; to share in eternity with Him, the angels, the archangels and all the company of heaven, and to be sent out in the power of the Holy Spirit to live and work to His praise and glory.

In my journey, I have experienced the healing power of Christ and the privilege of being a willing channel for that healing power in the world until that moment when, in His love for us He will give me the most perfect healing of all to carry me through death into life eternal.

Until then, my journey goes on, and the need for forgiveness remains a daily need, as does the need to 'strive afresh against the foe' and with the help and guidance of Almighty God to rid my life of those things which are a hurt to Him and my neighbour, so that my relationships with them both may be according to His will.

It is my prayer for you all, that your journey will not only lead you to find yourselves, but more important still, the One Who loves you with that love which even death itself could not and cannot destroy. That love, peace and healing which the world can never give; that love peace and healing which will bring you fulfilment here and now and enable you to look forward in confident expectation to the love, joy, peace and healing of heaven. That love, peace and healing which will bring you to stand before Jesus, not only as your Judge, but also as your Saviour and your Friend.

Several years ago, when visiting Joan and Ted Hubbard dear Christian friends of ours in Bourton-on-the-water, I read Catherine Marshall's book, 'Meeting God at every turn', in which I found these words which so impressed me that I wrote them in my prayer book and I want to share them with you now,

Reckon without God?
To do so would be as nonsensical as ignoring the sun as we watch a shifting pattern of sunlight and shadow on the ground.

Reckon without God?
We'd better not, not in any area of life, if we are serious about knowing reality and about achieving our full potential. For our God never considers our work as merely a way to earn a living - so much an hour, so much a year. He has given each of us the gift of life with a specific purpose in view. To Him, work is a sacrament, even what we consider unimportant, mundane work, when done "as unto the Lord", it can have eternal significance.

It is therefore important to Him that we discover what our particular aptitudes and talents are; then that we use those talents to His glory and their maximum potential during our all too brief time on earth.

For each of us, He does have a plan.
What joy to find it and even out of our helplessness, let Him guide us to its fulfilment.

And finally, I leave you with a thought inspired by, and including, some of the closing lyrics of 'Les Misérables' - the Musical.

In these pages you will find my last confession,
Read it well, when I perhaps am sleeping,
It's the story of a walk through life with Jesus,
The One Who gave His life for me and has me in His keeping:
Trust in Him, and chains will never bind you,
And your grief at last you'll leave behind you,
Lord in Heaven, pour out on us your mercy,
Forgive us all our trespasses and lead us to your glory.
Take His hand, He'll lead you to Salvation,
In His love, for His love is everlasting,
And remember this truth that once was spoken,
To love another person, is to see the face of God.

APPENDIX

DEEP HARMONY

During the time I suffered from deep depression, I went through a period when I found it extremely helpful to express my thoughts in verse. In so doing, I also discovered within myself a real sense of the nearness of God that I cannot explain, but which in itself became clear in the verses as they progressed and resulted in this trilogy that it seems right to include under the above heading.

THE ETERNAL HANDS

Just think of those Eternal hands,
Held out, when time was begun,
To bring to birth, Sun, Moon, and Earth,
Through the Word, the Beloved Son.

Almighty and ever loving God,
You must have known, even then,
How your world, so rich and beautiful,
Would suffer in the hands of men.

It could have been so different Lord,
Had they only trusted you,
But instead, they knew best, or so they thought,
And so ate of that fruit their due.

For the tree of the knowledge of good and bad,
Was forbidden them in your love,
And instead you offered them the Tree of Life,
With its fruit of Heaven above.

The choice was theirs, and they made it Lord,
And you knew that the 'apple' would kill,
But you hadn't made them like puppets on strings,
Having given them the gift of freewill.

So the die was cast on that early morn,
Sin had triumphed, and man was a slave,
In the sweat of his brow he would earn his bread,
Till returning to dust in his grave.

And what of the rest of creation Lord?
You had given it into man's hand,
It too, must suffer the same awful fate,
Although it could not understand.

When I think of those Eternal hands,
That so lovingly had wrought,
A work so priceless and beautiful,
Brought by man's disobedience to nought.

Then I too, marvel at your love O Lord,
That you should hold out to man,
In the face of eternal punishment,
A wondrous redemption plan.

For you so loved the world you had made,
That you sent your Son - The Word,
To be the Saviour, Friend and Lord,
Of all who really cared.

His coming, no fanfare heralded,
For His was a lowly birth,
Yet it spoke, as it still speaks, of Glory on High,
And peace to men on earth.

In that humble home in Nazareth,
With His Mother and Joseph to care,
He grew in stature, in wisdom and grace,
And in all things completed His share.

From an early age, He knew that He
His Father's work must do,

So that the will, which in Him was found,
Might be found in others too.

Think now of those Eternal hands,
Held up on high to bless,
All who to their Saviour turn,
From the depth of their trespasses.

See how those hands as they beckon
To the sinner in his plight,
Bring promise of deliverance,
Out of darkness into light.

See how the sick, the blind, the lame,
For healing to the Saviour came,
One, brought by four of his friends, good folk,
Heard Jesus say, 'Get up and walk'!

Even the dead were within His call,
And restored to life again,
Like Lazarus; a maiden small;
And the Son of the Widow of Nain.

Herein was love, there was no doubt,
It was there for all to see,
So they made Him King and gave Him a throne
Of wood on Calvary.

And there, as they raised Him up on high,
Pierced with anguish through and through,
He even prayed 'Father forgive them
For they know not what they do'!

When I think of those Eternal hands,
Nailed there by the sins of men,
And I see that those arms are open still,
Then I take heart again.

For I know that there, as He died on that tree,
He paid the price, that we might be free,
And those arms opened wide for all to see,
Beckon 'all who are weary, come to me'.

Those Eternal hands are outstretched still,
For Him, no cross, nor grave could kill,
And now from on high where the Saviour reigns,
Those same healing hands would remove my chains.

Lord, how I need to take them in mine,
Lord, how I long for your presence divine,
So take now my hands, my life and my love,
And fashion them in your way, for heaven above.

THE FACE OF THE SAVIOUR

There's a picture of the Saviour,
Of a look on His face as He turned,
To look upon Simon Peter,
How the heart of that man must have burned.

For Peter the Rock had denied his Lord,
When the moment of trial had come,
'I know not the man', he had cursed and had sworn
Once, twice, three times in sum.

And when the cock crowed that early morn,
The one who his watch should have kept,
When he saw the look on the Saviour's face,
Went out from His presence and wept.

It is easy to scorn him for his deed,
And say we would have done better,
But how often have we been as guilty as he,
Right down to the very last letter?

So let us look at the Saviour's face,
To see what we find in His gaze,
To speak to us in our pilgrimage,
As it moves on from phase to phase.

There's a peace in the face of the Saviour,
That the world can never give,
For it is the gift of the Saviour alone,
To those who trust Him to live.

There's a smile on the face of the Saviour,
For all who to Him come,
For healing, for pardon and blessing,
The blind and the deaf and the dumb.

That is why there's rebuke in the Saviour's face,
For those who turned children away,
When it was His will, as indeed it is still,
That they, in His presence should stay.

We find joy too, in the Saviour's face,
When faith He finds in a few,
Like that in the Roman Centurion,
And the Syrophoenician non-Jew.

But there's grief in the face of the Saviour,
When no faith He finds in the way,
When men hate Him, scorn and rebuke Him,
And ridicule all He may say.

And what of the pain in the Saviour's face,
From the nails and the crown of thorns,
Placed there by men's sins, your sins and mine,
And by Him on Calvary borne.

That's why there's a tear on the Saviour's face,
As there was at Lazarus's tomb,

For those who choose death instead of life,
And instead of God's presence, deep gloom.

But then there's hope in the Saviours face,
That those who reject Him are few,
While those who trust will be many,
Men, women and children too.

For there's glory too in the Saviour's face,
And in it all may share,
It brings joy and peace and freedom,
To all who really care.

Will we bring joy to the Saviour's face,
When Him at life's end we will see,
For to share in eternity forever with Him,
Is His longing for you and for me.

Inspired by the painting by Herbert Beecroft depicting the words, "The Lord turned and looked straight at Peter. Then Peter remembered."
(St Luke chapter 22 verse 61)

THE BEAUTY OF HOLINESS

Often, when life its toll has taken,
Or when doubt my faith has shaken,
Back to its rest, my heart it goes,
Where time into Eternity flows.

It was here as a babe in arms I was brought,
In response to all that the Saviour taught,
That folk the world over, His disciples would be,
When they answer His call of 'follow me'.

It was there at the font that I became
A member of Christ, when they gave me my name,
The Child of God too, in the fullest sense,
With Heaven as my inheritance.

A new name, a new start, a new life was mine,
Through the death of God's Son, my Saviour Divine,
And from that moment on, the devil must start
To find other refuge outside of my heart.

As the child of God, it was here I was brought,
By parents and friends and gently taught,
To pray and to worship in God's family,
Of His Kingdom in Heaven, a facsimile.

But then came the time my full part to play
In that family's life, I could not delay,
To confirm for myself those promises three,
Made long before by Godparents for me.

Kneeling near to where the Lectern stands,
I received God's Spirit, through laid on hands,
His Seven-fold Gifts were on me outpoured,
As my heart in thanksgiving, to Heaven soared.

And now as a member of God's family true,
I knew the duty that I must do,
In attending on Sundays, one by one,
The Service of Holy Communion.

It is here in the beauty of holiness,
That I feel the warmth of my Saviour's caress,
Here, where time and eternity meet,
I find the answer to make life complete.

When the Saviour's Body and His Blood,
Broken and poured out on Calvary's wood,
To me are given through Bread and Wine,
That I may partake in His life divine.

No words of mine can ever explain
What I feel, as I meet Him again and again,
And how I long, as I'm sure He does too,
That you will find here, a message for you.

A message which says 'there's a welcome for you'
Where you will find peace and forgiveness too,
So seek for the Lord, while He may be found,
And in beauty of holiness, your faith too, will abound.

ACKNOWLEDGEMENTS

Biblical quotations from the New International Version, are reproduced by kind permission of Hodder and Stoughton Limited.

The words of the hymn 'We have a gospel to proclaim' are reproduced by kind permission of their Author © The Revd. Canon E.J.Burns.

The words of 'My Forever Friend' are reproduced by kind permission of their Author Mr. Charlie Landsborough © 1994 Wilma Publishing/Valentine Music Group Ltd.

Extracts from and references to 'Les Misērables' by Alain Boublil and Claude Michel Schönberg, English Lyrics by Herbert Kretzmer, are by the kind permission of Alain Boublil (Overseas) Limited.

Extracts from 'Journey to Wholeness' by Bishop Morris Maddocks, published by Triangle SPCK, are by kind permission of SPCK.

Extracts from 'Meeting God at every turn' by Catherine Marshall and 'Discipleship' and 'Fear no evil' both by David Watson, are reproduced by kind permission of Hodder and Stoughton Limited.

Hymns 162, 428 and 506, either whole or in part from Complete Mission Praise, © Peter Horrobin, Greg Leavers and London and Nationwide Missions (1999). Reprinted by permission of HarperCollins Publishers Ltd.

The Prayer 'Lord Jesus when we fall' by Andrew Moore © Copyright 1977 Kevin Mayhew Ltd., Buxhall, Stowmarket, Suffolk, IP14 3 BW. Used by permission from 'The Way of the Cross', Licence Nr.408072.

Extracts from 'The Gospel of John Vol.2' (The Daily Study Bible), and 'Ambassador for Christ', both by William Barclay, are reproduced by kind permission of the Publishers Saint Andrew Press.

For your notes and references